MANAGEMENT CONTROL:
Planning, Control, Measurement, and Evaluation

KENNETH J. EUSKE
Naval Postgraduate School

MANAGEMENT CONTROL:
Planning, Control,
Measurement,
and Evaluation

ADDISON-WESLEY PUBLISHING COMPANY
Reading, Massachusetts • Menlo Park, California
London • Amsterdam • Don Mills, Ontario • Sydney

This book is in the
Addison-Wesley Paperback Series in Accounting

Consulting Editor
William J. Bruns, Jr.

Library of Congress Cataloging in Publication Data

Euske, K. J. (Kenneth J.)
 Management control.

 (Addison-Wesley paperback series in accounting)
 Bibliography: p.
 1. Management.   I. Title.   II. Series.
 HD31.E835   1983   658.4'01   83-12236
 ISBN 0-201-10494-6

Copyright © 1984 by Addison-Wesley Publishing Company, Inc.

All rights reserved. No part of this publication may be reproduced, stored in a retrieval system, or transmitted, in any form or by any means, electronic, mechanical, photocopying, recording, or otherwise, without the prior written permission of the publisher. Printed in the United States of America. Published simultaneously in Canada.

ISBN 0-201-10494-6
ABCDEFGHIJ-AL-89876543

To Nancy, Viola, and Bobby

EDITOR'S FOREWORD

The environment for accounting has undergone revolutionary changes in the last decade. Demand for accountability by managers of both public and private organizations has risen significantly. Electronic data transmission, storage, and processing and other information technologies have developed to allow accountants to use methods and processes that would have been considered impossible, or uneconomical, just a few years ago. At the same time, new quantitative methods for solving accounting problems have been developed, and the behavioral sciences have suggested that the impact of accounting goes well beyond the systems and reports, which are the most visible product of the accountant's work.

The speed with which these developments have occurred has made it difficult for teachers and students of accounting, and for managers and accountants themselves, to keep their knowledge up-to-date. New solutions to problems, and sometimes even new kinds of accounting problems themselves, are not treated in many textbooks. In addition, problems and solutions often cross boundaries between what were once considered separate disciplines of study. The student or manager seeking a learning aid in an era of change will frequently be frustrated. In many respects, materials which have been available do not reflect either the new developments or the unprecedented opportunities for creative thinking and problem solving which accounting presents.

Each book in this Addison-Wesley Series treats a new development or subject that has not been widely treated in textbooks that are widely available. In addition, because each book concentrates on a single set of problems, methods, or topics in accounting, each provides comprehensive coverage in an economical form. The Series was conceived to help all who work with or process accounting information, all of whom must continue to learn in order to keep pace with the changes which are occurring. Each book has been carefully developed by an outstanding scholar.

Books in this Series were prepared in the belief that the evaluation of accounting and its importance to managers will continue, and with faith that books are an effective means to assist all who are interested to participate in the developments which will take place in the future. Our goal has been to improve the practice and processes of accounting, and to help all who use accounting information to do so more effectively.

William J. Bruns, Jr.
Professor of Business
Administration
Harvard University

PREFACE

The goal of this monograph is to help the reader develop an understanding of management control systems. To achieve this goal it is important to understand the key variables that affect and are affected by management control systems and to be able to identify why a particular management control system either facilitates or frustrates the achievement of desired results. I have presented a number of ideas that can either make or break a management control system. They may seem disparate. Indeed as a student of the subject, I was often confused by the apparently disjointed topics that are considered important to understanding management control systems. This monograph explains those relationships.

The book is divided into seven chapters. Chapter One provides a framework for analyzing management control systems and is the motivation for each of the subsequent chapters. The case is made that the definitive model of management control does not exist. Therefore the model presented in this book is descriptive and is meant to help the student understand what drives the operation of management control systems.

Chapters Two, Three, and Four deal with planning and goals, control, and evaluation, respectively. The purpose of these chapters is to demonstrate how these topics relate to management control systems. Each chapter is designed to give the student an exposure to a specific topic and an understanding of the broad range of ideas relating to it.

Chapter Five, Measurement, and Chapter Six, Theory, are perhaps the most interesting chapters in the book. They form the core from which the different views of management control are developed. However, to fully appreciate the relevance of these two chapters, a basic understanding of management control systems is required. Because this book may be the reader's first formal exposure to management control systems, I have placed measurement and theory near the end; either one or both chapters may be skipped and the remaining parts of the book will remain meaningful. If the reader has had a formal introduction to management control systems, reading the chapters in the order of One, Six, Five, Two, Three, Four, and Seven may prove to be the most useful.

Chapter Seven ties together the ideas found in the previous chapters.

The bibliography is extensive for two reasons. First, I wanted to keep the book concise. However, much has been written on the subject matter discussed in this monograph. To achieve the brevity desired, I selected and discussed the particular works that helped me understand the topic of interest. Second, I wanted to provide the reader a ready bibliography on a wide range of management-control related literature. Therefore other writers presenting different explanations of the same phenomena are referenced in the bibliography. Readers may find these useful as well.

I am grateful to a number of individuals for their help with this monograph. Nancy Euske and Steven Funk read and criticized early drafts, while Dan Boger, Glenn Lindsey, and William Haga read selected chapters, pointing out inaccuracies and other assorted problems. Additionally, I would like to thank the five reviewers—Shahid Ansari, Robert Anthony, William Bruns, James Fremgen, and Cliff Rock—who read the final draft, providing insightful comments to strengthen it. I would like to thank Jennifer Frick and Jason Carmona for their early involvement in developing this manuscript and Linda Schmidt, who prepared the final draft. Finally, I owe a debt of thanks to my students in my course, "Planning and Control," at the Naval Postgraduate School. To a large extent they are the people who inspired this book, helped organize the contents, and provided many of the examples and anecdotes. Obviously whatever flaws remain are my responsibility alone.

Carmel, California K. J. E.
October 1983

CONTENTS

Preface	ix

1 The Use of Management Control Systems — 1
Planning and Goals — 7
Control — 7
Evaluation — 7
Measurement — 8
Background — 10

2 Planning and Goals — 13
Planning — 14
  Level of Detail and Degree of Specificity — 16
  Planning for the Unexpected — 17
  Correspondence between Plan and Outcome — 18
  Differences between Planning and Control — 18
  Planning—Structure and Process — 19
  Anthony's Model — 22
  Strategic versus Tactical Planning — 23
  Inhibitors to Planning — 23
  Summary of Planning — 26

Goals — 27
  Types of Goals — 27
  Goal Setting — 28

	Bargaining Model	28
	Problem-Solving Model	28
	Dominant Coalition Model	29
	Articulation of Goals and Objectives	29
3	**Control**	**31**
	Types of Control	33
	Directing or Correcting	33
	Individual, Group, or Organizational	36
	The Control Process	36
	Reciprocity of Control	43
	Reaction to Control	45
	Achieving Control	48
4	**Evaluation**	**51**
	Evaluation Defined	53
	The Measurement Definition	53
	The Congruence Definition	54
	The Judgment Definition	58
	Types of Evaluation	60
	What to Evaluate	60
	Effort	64
	Effectiveness	64
	Adequacy	64
	Efficiency	65
	Process	65
	When to Evaluate	65
	Context Evaluation	67
	Input Evaluation	67
	Process Evaluation	68
	Product Evaluation	68
	Levels or Types of Evaluation	68
	Purposes of Evaluation	68
	Evaluations Not Worth Doing	69

Evaluators—Inside or Outside	70
Accountants as Evaluators	71
Evaluation and Control	71
Summary	73

5 Measurement — 75

Elements of Measurement and the Measurement Process	78
Scaling	78
Nominal Scale	79
Ordinal Scale	80
Interval Scale	80
Ratio Scale	82
Meaningfulness	83
Specification	84
Standards	85
Reliability	86
Validity	86
Types of Measurement	86
Developing Measurement Systems	87
Functional Fixation	89
Summary	90

6 Theory — 93

Explaining Reality	95
A Second Explanation	97
Syntactics	97
Semantics	98
Pragmatics	98
Empirical and Nonempirical Sciences	99
The Relationship	101
The Case for Intuition	102
Theory Formulation	103

The Verification Process	104
Decision Making	105
Theory Verification and Measurement	107
Summary	107

7 The Design of Management Control Systems   109

Design Considerations	111
Goals and Objectives	111
Attributes Measured	113
Manipulation	114
Timing	115
Bottom Up and Top Down	116
Outside Support	116
The Designers	116
Line versus Staff Needs	117
External Reporting Needs	118
Resistance	118
The Management Control System and the Operating Environment	119
Summary	119
Bibliography	**121**
Author Index	**133**
Subject Index	**135**

MANAGEMENT CONTROL:
Planning, Control, Measurement, and Evaluation

Chapter One

THE USE OF MANAGEMENT CONTROL SYSTEMS

PLANNING AND GOALS
CONTROL
EVALUATION
MEASUREMENT
BACKGROUND

Possibly the best-known definition of management control is that "it is the process by which managers assure that resources are obtained and used effectively and efficiently in the accomplishment of the organization's objectives" (Anthony, 1965, p. 17). This definition emphasizes that the function of management control is to facilitate the accomplishment of organizational goals by implementing previously identified strategies. Holfstede provides another very useful definition of management control, defining it "as a pragmatic concern for results, obtained through people" (1981, p. 193). The value of Hofstede's definition lies in its emphasis on three important aspects of management control: pragmatism, results, and people.

Briefly let us consider these in turn. First, management control is pragmatic. It is not an abstract description or process. Management control is meant to achieve goals within the specific environment in which it operates. Second, management control focuses on results, which are defined as reaching the goals or objectives both of the specific operation at hand and of the larger organization. Third, and possibly the most important aspect of management control, is that it is concerned with people in organizations. People are the reason management control has significance and ultimately it is they that make an organization successful or not. However, our ability to accurately predict or control human behavior is not well developed. Management control, therefore, is less than a science.

This chapter presents a model to describe management control and to provide a framework for the discussion that follows in succeeding chapters. The term *model,* as used in this text, is defined as an abstraction of some phenomenon or idea. Six main elements and two types of relationships between the elements are depicted in the model presented in Fig. 1.1. The elements of the model are:

1. *Goals and objectives*—statements of organizational purpose or desired achievement, for example, that a hospital will provide comprehensive health care in some geographic area.
2. *Situational contingencies*—characteristics of an organization, such as size, or factors that have an impact on an organization, such as the occurrence of specific health hazards in the geographic area.
3. *Components of the management control system*—elements that make up the management control system, such as the number of reports, the relative degree of detail of those reports, and the length of the reporting cycle.
4. *Performance*—accomplishments of the organization, for example, comprehensive health care provided by a hospital.
5. *Outputs to be assessed*—specific elements of performance that are identified and incorporated into the management control system, such as outpatient surgery services provided.
6. *Attributes measured or performance measures*—characteristics of outputs that are identified for purposes of evaluation, for example, the number of outpatient operations performed.

The relationships are either desired or circumstantial. The desired relationships, depicted by the solid lines in Fig. 1.1, are as follows:

1. The selection and design of the components or characteristics of a management control system are influenced by both the situational contingencies in the environment in which the system operates and the goals and objectives of the organization.
2. The components of the management control system in turn lead to performance desired by the organization.
3. The performance is the means to accomplish the goals and objectives of the organization.

4   The Use of Management Control Systems

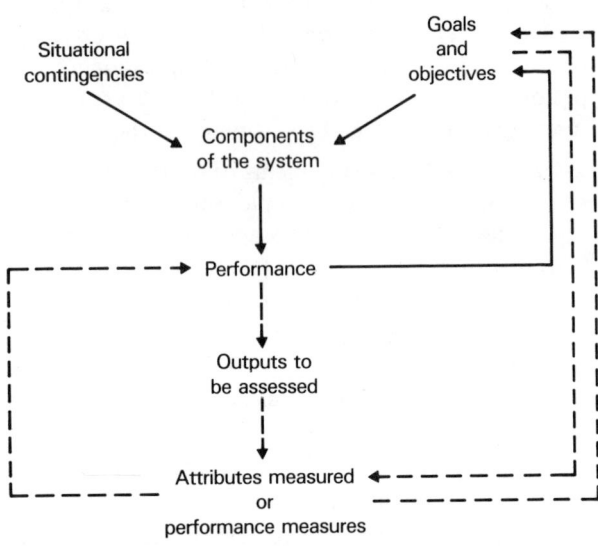

Figure 1.1   A Model of Management Control Systems

Key: Desired relationships ———
Circumstantial relationships — — — —

Circumstantial relationships, also result from this chain. These relationships, depicted by the dotted lines in Fig. 1.1, can be described as follows:

1. Identifying and measuring performance per se is more complex a task than can be accomplished in most cases. Therefore, some smaller set of outputs are chosen to be assessed.
2. Attributes or performance measures are then defined for the outputs. These measures are assessments not of performance per se but of attributes of the outputs of performance.
3. The performance measures then become the means for evaluating whether goals and objectives are being achieved, either for an organization or for an individual within an organization.
4. The goals and objectives in turn influence which particular measures of the assessed outputs will be used for such an evaluation.

5. Because rewards and sanctions are tied to the performance measures, resources are allocated to ensure that the performance measures are at the desired level. The performance measures then come to be viewed as performance per se; that is, the measures used are believed to be true performance.

The ideas represented in the model have been expressed by other writers. Anthony (1965) addresses these same general issues. Ansari (1977) presents a model that focuses on the interaction of behavioral and informational variables in a control system. Brace et al. (1980) have a model that deals with similar issues. Lebas's (1980) model focuses on the same issues as those presented here, but is more complex.

The model presented here is simple, but not simplistic. It can be used to analyze both individual and organizational behavior as it relates to management control. The model depicts the way the process of setting goals and objectives interrelates with situational contingencies to affect the characteristics of the management control system. A management control system is designed to facilitate performance. Specific outputs are identified, and measures of these outputs are generated that in turn are used within the management control system. Each step depicted in the model—planning, control, evaluation, and measurement—contributes to the operation of the management control system. Planning occurs in generating specifications of how the organization is intended to affect the future. The goals and objectives are a major statement of those intended effects. Control happens when components of the management control system are used to insure that the outputs are generated. Evaluation occurs as attributes of the outputs are appraised in terms of the performance as specified by the goals and objectives. Measurement is a necessary condition for planning, control and evaluation to occur.

Planning is primarily concerned with the relationship between preconditions (such as goals and objectives) and causal factors (such as components of the management control system). Control is primarily concerned with the relationship between causal factors and actual effects (the attributes measured of the outputs). Evaluation is primarily concerned with the relationship between actual effects and desired effects (such as performance as specified by the goals and objectives). Figure 1.2 depicts these relationships. However, each of the three processes requires the other two to occur as well. Some control is necessary to insure that a plan will result from the process. The plan in turn must be evaluated minimally for its reasonableness. Control and evaluation each necessitate the use of the other two processes. To put it another way, any process requires planning, control, and evaluation—even planning, control, and evaluation.

Though various models of management control exist, there is no definitive model of management control. One reason for this is that the theory on which all of the models are based is deficient. The models cannot consistently predict actual outcomes based on specific inputs. The elements of the models and the relationship of those elements are not fully understood. Any particular element or relationship could be questioned and possibly diagrammed differently because of competing explanations for what happens. The model used in this text and the other models cited previously are examples of various attempts to tie together disparate information that relates to management control systems. Each of the models cited is useful and each will be improved, corrected, or replaced by a better model founded on a sounder theory (Kuhn, 1970). To fully understand the usefulness of a particular model, an appreciation

Figure 1.2 Relationship between Planning, Control, and Evaluation and the Model of Management Control Systems

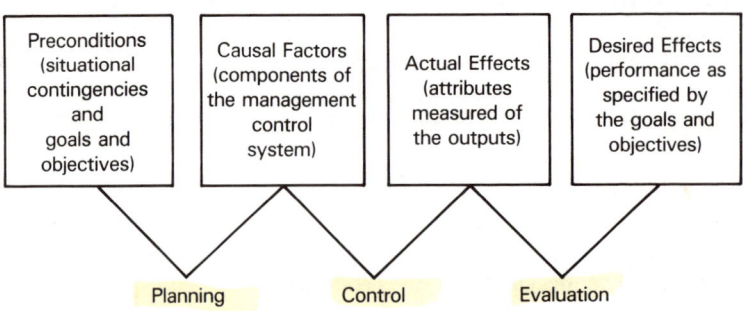

Source: Adapted from E. A. Suchman, *Evaluative Research* (New York: Russell Sage Foundation, 1967), p. 173.

for what defines a theory and how it is developed is useful. The importance of theory to the understanding, design, and implementation of management control systems is discussed in Chapter Six.

PLANNING AND GOALS

The goals and objectives of the organization are givens for the management control system, which addresses how best they can be accomplished. The specificity of the goals and objectives affects the success of a management control system. Poorly specified goals and objectives will create difficulty because of the resulting uncertainty and ambiguity. However, precisely stated goals and objectives can be equally problematic. The specific statements of purpose will tend to be short run (Bromiley and Euske, 1983). Though the specific short-run statements of purpose may be met, longer-run statements of purpose may be ignored. For instance, consider the manager who has done a fine job in the short run but who, a closer look reveals, has avoided long-run decisions. Why? One reason could be that the planning horizon and resulting goals and objectives were short term. What does this mean to the organization? The obvious result is that short-term performance is achieved but there may not be a conscious effort to achieve long-term success (Rappaport, 1981). The planning and goal-setting process is discussed further in Chapter Two.

CONTROL

What is necessary to achieve control? Even more basic, what is control? What are the major elements of a control system? If management control systems are to be developed, a specific understanding of control must exist. Chapter Three addresses aspects of control that are relevant to management control systems.

EVALUATION

The use of information from a management control system for purposes of evaluation also affects the management control system. For instance, as part of the management control system in most accounting firms, engagements are budgeted with a specific amount of hours to accomplish the specific task. The staff accountants who are sent into the field are aware of the time budgeted to complete the task. Deviations from the time budget are important information for the control, use, and pricing of resources within the organization. Staff accountants are evaluated in part according to their ability to stay within the budgeted hours for the specific output desired. The application of this input/output or efficiency measure to individuals prompts the staff accountants to want to report hours that are within the budget. The staff accountants then donate unreported time to the organization to make sure the work is done well and under budget. The unreported time makes it appear that less resources are required to complete an engagement than is actually the case. The process of evaluation for the staff accountant has thus affected the management control process for the entire organization.

Information from management control systems will be used for evaluation, both of individuals and operations. Therefore, what should be evaluated and how? When should performance be evaluated, such that useful information will be provided both for evaluation and within the management control system? These evaluation issues are discussed in Chapter Four.

MEASUREMENT

One example of a simple control system, used at a very low level of resource management in the organization, is illustrated by a manufacturing company that had a scrap yard about two miles from its production plant. The process at the production plant generated scrap metal in addition to its main output. The scrap, which included such expensive metals as stainless steel, molybdenum, copper, titanium, and beryllium, was hauled to the scrap yard, then sorted and sold to scrap dealers. Because the scrap was valuable, a control system was installed to provide reasonable assurance that the scrap would reach the yard without any of it being pilfered.

Under this system, trucks that transported the scrap from the production plant to the scrap yard were tagged as they went out the gate. The gate guards noted on the tags the time that the driver left the production plant; the time was again listed when the driver entered the scrap yard. The time it took the driver to go the two miles was recorded for control purposes. If a tag indicated an inordinate amount of time for the trip, additional investigation was made. The measure served as an indicator of the stated objective—to minimize scrap loss from plant to yard. But this control system was based only on time; the trucks were not weighed at either end of the trip. One can infer that the designers of the system assumed that the time control eliminated the potential for a driver to make a quick stop and remove part of the load. However, without weighing the vehicle, there is no way to know whether this assumption was correct. The company was not measuring a full load of material brought in by the driver. If for some reason part of the load was lost, there was nothing within the control system to motivate the driver to stop. In fact, if the driver wished to avoid attention, stopping would be counterproductive. If the driver was conscientious and stopped, the attention of management might be drawn to the lengthy trip time. The system measured on-time behavior, which was not performance. However, as stated earlier, what is measured is rarely performance itself but some specific attribute relating to the performance.

Another example of this phenomenon is the drilling of oil wells in the Soviet Union. Workers' productivity was measured by meters of oil well drilled rather than by how much oil was located. What happened? Many meters of oil well were drilled but not much oil was located. Why? The Soviets were not rewarding oil-finding behavior but well-drilling behavior. As Kerr (1975) argues, the behavior rewarded is the behavior that can be expected. There are other examples from the Soviet Union. Productivity at sheet glass factories was measured by the tons of output produced. As a result the sheet glass factories produced very heavy and thick sheet glass, which was not very desirable. However, by changing the measure to square meters of output the tendency would be to produce glass with a larger surface area but thinner than it ought to be (Nove, 1977). Both tons of output and square meters of output are attributes of output that relate to performance. However, neither of the attributes captures the essence of performance. The management control system did get results, but in a broad sense control was not achieved—the desired behaviors were not elicited from the workers. What can be done to identify attributes and measures of attributes that relate to performance in a desired manner? How can the manager be certain that the desired information is contained in the numbers? Chapter Five deals with questions of assigning numbers to attributes and what must be considered to develop meaningful and useful measurement systems.

BACKGROUND

As the previous discussion indicates, management control deals with complex processes involving many entities and relationships. Conceptualizing the complexities is difficult but is made easier by using systems theory. For those who have not been exposed to systems theory and thinking there are a number of excellent works, some of which are listed at the end of the chapter. The particular definitions of terms used in this text are drawn primarily from Boulding (1956), Hall and Fagen (1956), Hardin (1968), and Kast and Rosenzweig (1972).

SUGGESTED READINGS

Ansari, Shahid L. An integrated approach to control system design. *Accounting, Organizations and Society*, 1977, *2*(2), 101-112.

Anthony, Robert N. *Planning and Control Systems: A Framework for Analysis*. Boston: Harvard University, 1965.

Baker, Frank (Ed.). *Organizational Systems: General Systems Approach to Complex Organizations*. Homewood; Ill.: Richard D. Irwin, 1973.

Berrien, F. Kenneth. *General and Social Systems*. New Brunswick, N.J.: Rutgers University Press, 1968.

Bertalanffy, Ludwig Von. *General System Theory: Foundations, Development, Applications*. New York: George Braziller, 1968.

Boulding, Kenneth E. General systems theory—The skeleton of science. *Management Science*, 1956, *2*, 197-208.

Brace, Paul K., Robert Elkin, Daniel D. Robinson, and Harold I. Steinberg. *Reporting of Service Efforts and Accomplishments*. Stamford, Conn.: Financial Accounting Standards Board, 1980.

Buckley, Walter (Ed). *Modern Systems Research for the Behavioral Scientist*. Chicago: Aldine Publishing Company, 1968.

Churchman, C. West. *The System Approach*. New York: Dell Publishing Company, 1968.

Dermer, Jerry. *Management Planning and Control Systems*. Homewood, Ill.: Richard D. Irwin, 1977.

Kast, Fremont E. and James E. Rosenzweig. General systems theory: Applications for organization and management. *Academy of Management Journal*, December 1972, *15*(4), 447–465.

Miller, James G. The nature of living systems. *Behavioral Science*, July 1971, *16*, 278–301.

Pfeffer, Jeffrey and Gerald R. Salancik. *The External Control of Organizations: A Resource Dependence Perspective*. New York: Harper & Row, 1978.

Chapter Two

PLANNING AND GOALS

PLANNING
Level of Detail and Degree of Specificity
Planning for the Unexpected
Correspondence between Plan and Outcome
Differences between Planning and Control
Planning—Structure and Process
Anthony's Model
Strategic versus Tactical Planning
Inhibitors to Planning
Summary of Planning
GOALS
Types of Goals
Goal Setting
   Bargaining Model
   Problem-Solving Model
   Dominant Coalition Model
Articulation of Goals and Objectives

This chapter presents a discussion of the planning process, including goal setting. This discussion will help to identify the difference between planning and control. Though the distinction may be more arbitrary than real, it will help explain what control is not. As discussed in Chapter One, both planning and goals and control affect management control. Through planning and the setting of goals the desired achievements and behaviors are specified. In the model of management control systems in Fig. 1.1, the goals, along with the situational contingencies, are shown as influencing the selection and design of the components of the management control system.

Some writers in the field of planning and goal setting differentiate between goals and objectives, while other writers use these terms interchangeably. Some define objectives as long-term, value-laden purposes; others describe goals the same way. In this text the word *goals* refers to the long-term, value-laden concepts that the organization has identified as important; *objectives,* by contrast, are the short-term statements of purpose. For instance, one goal for a firm might be to be the leader in marketing laser optic devices. An objective might be the specific sales target for a given year.

PLANNING

This section describes the structure and process of planning and briefly presents the relationship of planning to control. The section ends with a discussion of factors that inhibit planning.

Newman defines planning as "deciding in advance what is to be done" (1951, p. 15). Ackoff expands on this idea of planning as anticipatory decision making, describing planning as "a process of deciding what to do and how to do it before the action is required" (1970, p. 2). Other definitions of planning have that same essential ingredient of a future state or time reference.

Planning is done within organizations to affect the behavior of an individual, a group, a department, an organization, or an economy. The purpose of a plan is to bring about behavior that leads to desired outcomes, whether the plan is developed by an individual or through a group process within the organization (Emery, 1969). According to Ackoff (1970), planning is done because sets of decisions exist that are too large to handle at once. The decisions are therefore divided into subsets that can be handled sequentially by a single body or simultaneously by a number of bodies.

One characteristic of the subsets of decisions is that they are interrelated. Each decision affects previous and subsequent decisions. Therefore, there is a need to continually review and revise every decision previously made in light of each new decision and vice versa. As Ackoff states, "planning is not an act but a process" (1970, p. 3); in other words, it does not have an endpoint. The moment the plan is apparently complete, the environment changes, and the plan is out of date. For instance, the development and introduction of a new product, service, or weapons system represents an original plan that has been reworked many times to bring the final output to fruition. The product review and development cycle in a firm such as Procter and Gamble and the weapon system development cycle within the Department of Defense both exemplify the need to develop a plan, test it against reality, and revise the plan to accommodate the new reality and prognosticated changes. The new toothpaste or weapon system that reaches the user will probably be much different from what was originally planned. Additionally, the product is not likely to meet the needs of the user in the current environment given that the current environment may be different from what was projected (Adler, 1966; Crawford, 1977). To say a plan is finished implies that the plan is being measured by a preselected criterion—a snapshot of one point in time. Completion is not implicit in a plan unless the environment can be held constant during the planning process.

The plan is also a means to produce one or more future states that are desired but that are not expected to occur unless selected actions are taken (Ackoff, 1970). Planning is a process by which opportunities can be identified and exploited and incorrect actions can be avoided or at least minimized. If there is no concern about what is going to happen, it follows that there is no reason to plan. Also, if the event is inevitable, there is no reason to plan to affect it. Plan for those things that are controllable. Do not worry about the things that are not. If the future cannot be affected, why try to marshal the resources to affect it? Attempting to plan the inevitable is a waste of resources.

However, planning is not always a process by which a desired state (goal) is identified and activities marshalled to achieve that desired state or goal. Sometimes planning is reactive; that is, if A occurs, X action will be taken. If B occurs, Y action will be taken. If it is cloudy tomorrow morning, wear a raincoat; if it is sunny, leave the raincoat at home. These if-then statements, better known as contingencies, complicate the planning process because for every *if* identified, a corresponding *then* must be prescribed. Some of the changes in the environment can be predicted, but there may be some minor variation from what was prognosticated, and the manager will have to take actions other than those specified in the contingency plan. The change may be minor—the sky is partly cloudy. Even if the change is minor, the contingency plan will not perfectly match reality. The manager (or planner) must try to anticipate a changing process. This is like trying to tell somebody the correct time. Time moves as you attempt to measure it. Recorded time messages give the time by anticipating its movement—"At the tone, the time will be ten o'clock, exactly." However, the tone itself takes time. Just as the exact time is impossible to identify, a plan is never complete.

Level of detail and degree of specificity

How detailed do plans need to be? Do all plans have to be detailed? What are the behaviors of concern? Are the intermediate steps important, or is the final outcome the only major concern? If the steps along the way are important, precise procedural plans must be developed that specify the steps; but if the final outcome or product is the concern, a more general declarative plan can be used (Emery, 1969; March and Simon, 1958). For example, the plan could specify that within one year market channels be developed in Europe and Japan by using specific agents in specific locations. As an alternative the plan could simply specify that the market channels be developed within one year. Regardless of whether the plan is procedural like the first, or declarative like the second, to lead to desired outcomes the plan must:

1. describe some actions and outcomes;
2. serve as a formal vehicle of communication (Emery, 1969).

The degree of specificity of the plan also relates to the degree to which operations are coupled or centralized. Less specific plans are more likely to be acceptable if operations are loosely coupled or integrated than if they are highly integrated. The closer the coupling between the operations, the more specific must be the plans to make the operation work. Organizing workers on an assembly line requires more specific planning of behavior than does organizing a team of salespersons on a car lot (Emery, 1969).

Planning is a key element in the process of an organization. Given the central role of planning, the manager can affect and change the organization by changing the planning system. The manager in the role of the planner is in essence a trainer, identifying and providing rewards for appropriate behaviors and extinguishing inappropriate behaviors (Emery, 1969).

Planning for the unexpected

An unexpected occurrence by definition is not going to be part of a plan (Ackoff, 1970). It is a nonsense statement to say that one can plan for the unexpected. The planners may develop contingency plans by specifying general possibilities, but the contingencies specified will be in a general form and at least anticipated, if not expected. For instance, the operating budget of an activity will be developed so that the facility can continue to operate under many conditions. Forecasts are made of possible resource utilization (for example, a high heat bill because of a severe winter). As key events pass (calendar dates in this example), the resource needs change and the resources can be reallocated. Note that the organization does not maintain the allocation scheme from the previous six months. The environment changes, so the priorities change, and the plan is amended to reflect this.

Contingency plans are useful if there is uncertainty. However, to deal with the unexpected, a process needs to be created ahead of time so that when the unexpected occurs, a means exists for adjusting to the situation. If this kind of process is in place, the decisions needed to respond to the unexpected are facilitated. Thus the output of the planning process is not a plan but a process (Ackoff, 1970). The only way to plan for the unexpected is to have a process that is responsive to whatever the situation is. From a planning standpoint, the process is the most important product. The process is the method for responding to the unexpected.

Correspondence between plan and outcome

The correspondence between the plan and the outcome of the plan depends on:

1. the realism of the model used to generate the plan;
2. the accuracy with which the basic planning data are predicted;
3. the fidelity with which the plan is carried out (Emery, 1969, p. 146).

If a plan is to work, the best possible model must be used with the best available data, and the plan must be adhered to. If quantitative techniques that lead to optimization can be used, that is fine. If not, satisficing is appropriate. As Ackoff (1970) points out, both are useful approaches that can complement each other in dealing with complex situations.

Differences between planning and control

How does planning differ from control? The plan is the means by which the manager intends to affect the future; control is the means by which the manager ensures that the plan functions. Planning is prescribing a behavior. The prescription can be for a relatively short period of time, and expressed as the annual or quarterly budget or for a longer period of time and expressed as a program intended to occur over a three- to seven-year period. Controlling is maintaining behavior within preselected parameters. Ackoff (1970) discusses designing decision-making procedures and organizing them so that the plan can be carried out. The design of the procedures for anticipating and detecting abnormalities in the system and bringing the system back to the desired state is control (Ackoff, 1970). Any good planning process has a control cycle. For instance, a quarterly budget is a plan as well as a means to control. As a plan it is expressed in dollars identifying future states. As a means to control, it represents parameters for measuring the appropriateness of behavior. Said another way, the budget is an output of the planning process and an input to the control process. Steiner (1969) describes control and planning as two separate activities but treats them as if they were inseparable. The manager cannot plan if there is no information indicating current status. On the other hand, the manager cannot control unless there is some plan that indicates the purpose of the control. The two are complementary activities.

Planning—structure and process

Planning has both a process and a structure. Emery (1969) discusses five "steps" in the planning process, and Ackoff (1970) divides the plan into five "parts." We will examine both of these schemes.

According to Emery, the first step in the planning process is to determine the values or primitive data to be used. The primitive data may be either historical or projected. The primitive data, basic data, or planning factors may vary in detail depending on the level and purpose of the plan. For short-run planning of operations the data will probably be very detailed, whereas for long-run planning, the information may be much more general. For instance, to plan for the number and size of road crews necessary to fill the potholes in the county roads, the number, size, and location of the potholes would be important information. However, to plan the appropriate level of growth for the county and its resulting transportation needs, data such as the predicted growth in regional population and national economic growth patterns would be important.

Emery's second step in planning is to manipulate the primitive planning data in order to determine the consequences of alternative plans. If planning is viewed as a means to affect future behavior, the primitive planning data are useful only if they are expected to affect some future outcomes. The identification of these outcomes is usually a key task of the planner. However, the alternatives may not be at all obvious. Given that only identified alternatives can be selected to lead to desired outcomes, the ability to identify those alternatives is a most important characteristic of a planner.

Emery's third step is to select the best plan from the alternatives. If there is one objective, the selection of the most suitable plan is facilitated. However, in most cases there is not one simple objective, but rather multiple objectives, and more likely than not uncertain consequences of the alternatives. Even if there were one objective, an optimal alternative may or may not be selected. Only if all possible alternatives and outcomes have been analyzed can the planner reasonably expect that the optimal alternative is selected. With only one simple objective, it is likely that neither all possible alternatives nor outcomes will be identified, much less analyzed. Therefore something less than an optimal decision will result. Multiple objectives foster the use of quantitative or qualitative techniques to manage the objectives. The planner may try to develop a utility function, collapsing all goals into a compound objective. Some simple function aggregating all of the objectives into a single index of some sort may be generated. Some technique such as a Delphi technique might be used to identify the most important objective. In any case, care must be taken that important detail is not eliminated along the way. As Emery points out, averaging or rounding can hide significant differences among alternatives. He presents the example of how rounding to the nearest million dollars can make two inventory alternatives indistinguishable when in fact they differ by almost half a million dollars.

Emery's fourth step is to translate the selected plan into a form for operational planning. Aggregation done for planning at a more strategic level might necessitate disaggregation for operational planning.

The fifth and last step in Emery's planning process is control of the plan. As previously stated, control is comparing actual results against the plan and taking the necessary actions. In general, the purpose of control is to encourage realistic planning and close adherence to the approved plan. Control guards against excessive deviations from the plan that could cause a breakdown in the coordination necessary to achieve the plan's objectives. Emery describes it thus:

> The identification and correction of deficiencies in the planning process provides the primary means by which the organization can achieve fundamental improvement through adaptation. . . . Adaptation can be viewed as a continuation of hierarchical control. Thus, if a serious deviation is signalled by the control system, replanning may call for the revision of not only the plan having the immediate deviation, but also the model from which the plan was derived (representing a higher-level plan). The model may be revised through such means as changes in its parameters or, more fundamentally, in its basic structure (1969, p. 142).

Ackoff (1970) describes five parts of a plan's structure: ends, means, resources, implementation, and control. The ends are the goals or objectives specified in the plan. The means represent the policies, programs, and procedures through which the goals and objectives are to be pursued. Resources represent the determination of the type and quantities of resources needed to carry out the plan and the means by which to acquire them. Implementation concerns designing the processes by which the plan will actually be carried out. Control is "design of a procedure for anticipating or detecting errors in, or failures of, the plan and for preventing or correcting them on a continuing basis" (Ackoff, 1970, p. 6). Both Emery and Ackoff include control as the last stage or part of planning. Such analyses emphasize the mutual dependence of planning and control. Consistent with the discussion and model presented in Chapter One in this text, control, though dependent on the planning process, is identified as a separate process.

Emery's "steps" and Ackoff's "parts" indicate a process and structure that are not any different from those utilized to do budgeting as described in an accounting text (see, for example, Fremgen, 1976; Horngren, 1982; Lynn and Freeman, 1974; and Shillinglaw, 1977) or by once-popular techniques, such as zero-base budgeting (Pyhrr, 1973). They are all simply applications of the decision-making process. Each is an elaboration on attempts to answer three basic questions (Dewey, 1910):

1. What is the issue or problem?
2. What are the alternatives?
3. Which alternative should be selected?

Anthony's model

The planning process is not necessarily concerned with budgets or money but rather with resources. Anthony's (1965) framework indicates the relevance of this distinction. In his model the planning and control process in an organization is divided into three levels: the strategic planning level, the management control level, and the operational control level.

Strategic planning is the process by which an organization decides on its goals and on the major avenues by which it will achieve those goals (Anthony and Herzlinger, 1980). Strategic planning is concerned with the placement of the organization in its future environment. Strategic planning, as its name implies, is of a more long-run nature than either management control or operational control, which are the vehicles by which information is fed back to ensure that the strategic plan is being carried out. Strategic planning functions as a means by which the organization analyzes its environment to find opportunities for itself (Bracker, 1980). Given the orientation of the strategic planning process, the information used in this process tends to be predictive and externally oriented. The data may or may not be financial; the data might be demographic or consist of many other types of information.

Management control is the process by which management assures that resources are acquired and utilized to accomplish organizational goals (Anthony and Herzlinger, 1980). Management control is a continuous, administrative, persuasive activity that has a relatively close time horizon and focuses on the entire organization. Therefore, information is needed that is compatible between one section of the organization and another. The medium generally used is financial information.

Operational control is the process of assuring that specific tasks are carried out effectively and efficiently (Anthony and Dearden, 1980). It is a rational, directive activity concerned with day-to-day operations. Planning is necessary at this level, but the focus will be on single-organization tasks or transactions, such as the number of welds to be made in a day or the number of vouchers to be posted in a day. The focus also will be on things, not money.

Strategic versus tactical planning

One traditional way to categorize planning is either as tactical or strategic. Ackoff (1970) distinguishes the two in three major dimensions: time, scope, and means and goals. A strategic plan, which might consider the time it takes to build a new plant, is long range. Time is usually of a shorter range in tactical planning, and the plan—for example, the purchase of a piece of equipment—is therefore easier to change. The scope in strategic planning tends to be broad, affecting many functions, while the scope in tactical planning tends to be narrower, affecting fewer functions but more comprehensively. Strategic planning is concerned with formulating goals and selecting means. In tactical planning, the goals are given but means may be selected. In general, tactical planning concerns the methods for carrying out the subcomponents of a strategic plan. Or, said simply, strategy determines what is to be accomplished, tactics determine how it is to be accomplished.

Inhibitors to planning

Hardin (1968) identifies eight preconditions that, if not met, inhibit the development of a plan:

1. Can it be shown, before instituting a plan, that all significant factors have been taken into account?
2. Have all possible interactions of factors been identified?
3. Can a vehicle for transition from one state to another be devised?

4. Has the reflexive effect of knowledge and planning on the actions of the planners and the plan been considered?
5. Does the reflexive effect of knowledge create a system of cycling?
6. Can the calculations and analyses be conducted quickly enough to respond to the discovery of new information?
7. Can individuals be persuaded to change?
8. Will the plan adopted have adequate self-correcting mechanisms built into it?

Can the preconditions be satisfied, or is planning generally inhibited? Let us examine the eight preconditions in greater detail.

First, can all of the significant factors that may affect the plan be identified? The larger the organization, the more variables involved, so the harder it probably will be to identify all of them. Two questions of concern are: (1) What variables are going to affect the plan? (2) Do the variables change with time? A family budget is a good example. Most people would probably agree that it is reasonably easy to predict a monthly family budget, but can a monthly budget be predicted for the next year or the year after that? How accurate will the budget be? More likely than not, it is easier to identify those things that affect a personal budget than those that will affect a large organization's budget. However, even in planning the family budget there is uncertainty. Both budgets require predicting the future and the factors involved. Will all of the factors be identified? Probably not.

Hardin's second precondition, identifying interactions of the factors, is perhaps more difficult than the first. Hardin questions whether all possible interactions can be identified. It might be useful to change Hardin's wording from "all possible" to read "all significant." It is doubtful that one could predict all the significant interactions between the factors. It is possible, however, to maintain a flexible process so that unpredicted interactions can be accommodated. From an information management point of view, flexibility requires building a modular system in which the pieces can be connected or disconnected without rebuilding the entire information system from the ground up. To design such a system the planner must know which variables may change and how they interact. The argument again raises the question: Can the interactions be predicted? Ackoff's (1970) view of planning may offer the answer. In his model the identification of alternatives and the potential changes to the plan are parts of a process that is beneficial for dealing with a changing environment. The process is similar to driving to the store: Though a plan may exist of how to get from point *A* to point *B*, each curve and traffic light must be handled on an individual basis.

Hardin's third precondition is that even if we can predict a new, better, and more stable system, we must devise a means of transition from the current state to the desired state. Beckhard and Harris (1977) have dealt with the question of transitions within organizations. As they point out and as Hardin argues, transitions are not easily devised or managed, particularly for large populations.

Preconditions 4 and 5 concern the reflexive effect of knowledge, that knowledge gained interacts with previous knowledge, potentially changing both the understanding of old and newly acquired knowledge. Does the act of planning result in a different understanding of current and possible future conditions, which in turn leads to a reinterpretation of existing plans? Here Hardin seems to be addressing the same question that Weick addresses by proposing that "plans are not a blueprint to future success but rather an interpretation of the past extended into the future" (Weick, 1969, p. 102). If this is so, is this planning or post hoc justification?

Hardin's sixth precondition is that the calculations must be carried out promptly to do any kind of planning. If planning is to be done in some precise way, the planner will have to take into account many variables. As Hardin points out, the computations may be astronomical, and there may not be enough time or computing power to plan in detail.

Hardin's seventh precondition—can we expect people to change—has been asked since time began. The best planning or goal-setting system does not guarantee that the individuals involved with the system will either accept the end or the means to achieve that end.

Hardin's last precondition is that there must be adequate self-correcting mechanisms built into the process. If the planners are planning an artificial system—in which events are contrived rather than naturally occurring—how can they be sure that the self-correcting mechanisms will produce the desired results?

As the eight preconditions indicate, and as discussed previously, attempting to develop *the* plan that prescribes behaviors for all possible contingencies is futile. Rather, what can be done is to design a planning process with feedback to maintain it. Phrased in terms of Ackoff's (1970) approach, since the future cannot be predicted accurately, the goal of planning is to have a process in place to respond to the changing environment.

Hardin's discussion is probably most interesting for the questions he poses. How can managers plan if they cannot identify the important factors? What if they can identify the significant interactions but cannot develop the transitions from one point to another? Asking and attempting to answer such queries provide the context for the planning process.

Summary of planning

If planners could see clearly into the future, they would not have to rely on the past. Since the future is unknown, the only means of foretelling it is to look back. The better or larger the data base, the more faith in the predicted numbers. However, to develop a large data base, older data must normally be used, and the older the data, the more irrelevant they are. On the other hand, instantaneous data are relevant but probably not sufficient to predict the future confidently. Somewhere between old and current data lies a workable mix. However, it is important to remember that this mix of data is a pragmatic "fix" to an essentially unsolvable problem.

Given that planning is based on the past, it is largely an attempt to correct past errors (Ackoff, 1970). Planning for new products or equipment is a good example. It is reasonable to assume that managers and planners want to see newly introduced products and equipment meet the goals for which they were developed. How does the manager help to insure success? By avoiding mistakes identified from past experience. Therefore, planning requires a knowledge of history. If there is no history, there is no basis for projecting the future.

It can be argued that corporate planners do not give proper attention to history. For instance, during the 1970s domestic automobile producers experienced a decline in their share of new automobile sales in America. This indicates that their planning staffs did not fully consider the changing preferences American consumers were exhibiting. How could the corporate planners overlook major changes in the environment? Whatever the answer, the point is that, even when hindsight identifies seemingly major factors in the environment that have affected the future, these factors are at times not properly incorporated into the planning process.

GOALS

This section begins by presenting types of organizational goals and then discusses goal-setting models. The last section analyzes articulation of goals.

Types of goals

Writers such as Hall (1975) indicate that the term *goals* is ambiguous. There are goals of an organization—those held by the dominant coalition within the organization; there are also goals for an organization—those held by members and nonmembers (Thompson, 1967). There are official goals—the stated goals of the organization; and there are operative goals—the real or actual goals of the organization (Perrow, 1961). Regardless of the type of goal, Hall points out that a goal has two critical elements:

1. A goal represents future attainments.
2. A goal represents an allocation of present efforts or commitments.

Goals represent a bridge between the allocation of resources currently available and resource availability at some future time.

Goal setting

Hall (1975) discusses three different models of goal setting: bargaining, problem solving, and coalition formation.

Bargaining model. The bargaining model is drawn from the work of Cyert and March (1963). The bargaining model assumes an organization in which numerous participants hold conflicting goals. According to Hall, three important assumptions in the model are that:

1. the participants in the organization are active;
2. the participants have conflicting demands;
3. the individuals or groups in the organization are independent.

To achieve their goals, the individuals negotiate with each other, making trade-offs or concessions until a satisfactory array of goals is agreed upon. The members of the organization try to achieve various goals through the use of compromise and "side payments." However, these side payments may not always perfectly fit the situation at hand because they may not be consistent with either the organization's policies or resources available at the moment. Second, the side payments may be stated in terms of desirable rather than possible outcomes. And third, the objectives may be stated nonoperationally so they will not conflict with any other operational objective.

Problem-solving model. The second model Hall discusses is the problem-solving model drawn from the work of Simon (1964). This model uses goals as a set of constraints within which courses of action are taken. The three major assumptions crucial to the model, as identified by Hall, are:

1. Policy commitments are made within a set of constraints or requirements that are known to the decision makers.
2. The constraints can be ranked, and a preferred set can be accommodated.
3. The goals of different individuals or groups can be satisfied simultaneously.

Within the model it is made clear that the administrative hierarchy is the one that makes the major decisions. Those outside the hierarchy may influence the decisions informally, but they never directly participate in the decisions. Therefore the model focuses on the input of the individuals who influence the decision process informally by the amount of information they present. No one's goals are ever completely satisfied, but a satisfactory course of action is nevertheless selected.

Dominant coalition model. The third model of goal determination that Hall discusses is the dominant coalition model (Perrow, 1961; Thompson, 1967; and Hill, 1969). In this model, it is assumed that the many groups of individuals making up an organization do not have sufficient power to act unilaterally. Therefore some kind of coalition or collective behavior is necessary to achieve the organization's goals. These coalitions result in a commonly agreed-on goal that the individuals pursue. Control is shared among the coalitions, and mutual agreement is required during the decision process.

Each of the three models demonstrates or attempts to demonstrate that goals can be set by individuals or coalitions or through some kind of organizational process. In each case the goals represent the output of a process to which many individuals have contributed.

Articulation of goals and objectives

Though one may presume that there is a link between the highest-level goals and the most specific objectives, goals at one level do not necessarily get translated into objectives at lower levels. For example, Box (1957), in discussing the idea of "evolutionary operations," describes how operations are designed with limited testing and background information. He argues that the organization could experiment with these ongoing operations to find out what it takes to make them deviate from stated operational parameters. Such testing and the resulting information could help identify how good the system really is. Box's idea has face validity. However, a supervisor would probably say, "What do you mean, you're going to experiment with my operation?," not wanting to see what is necessary to make it malfunction. Even though the goal is to create a better system, experimentation may not help the supervisors running specific departments. A supervisor's objectives are such that a disruption could adversely affect the evaluation of the department. Emery (1969) discusses this in terms of goals becoming disjointed. As the goals are filtered down through the organization, they are not articulated. Contact is lost between the bottom and top of the organization. Special emphasis must be placed on translating organizational goals into specific objectives at the operational level. Poorly articulated goals and objectives frustrate the design and operation of the management control system. As previously discussed, both the planning process and the control process are means to effect the translation. In the next chapter, control and its functions are discussed.

SUGGESTED READINGS

Ackoff, Russel L. *A Concept of Corporate Planning.* New York: Wiley-Interscience, 1970.

Emery, James C. *Organizational Planning and Control Systems.* London: MacMillan Company, 1969.

Lawler, Edward E., III, and John Grant Rhode. *Information and Control in Organizations.* Pacific Palisades, Calif.: Goodyear Publishing Company, 1976.

Livingstone, J. Leslie. *Managerial Accounting: The Behavioral Foundations.* Columbus, Ohio: Grid, 1975.

Lorange, Peter. *Corporate Planning: An Executive Viewpoint.* Englewood Cliffs, N.J.: Prentice-Hall, 1980.

Perrow, Charles. The analysis of goals in complex organizations. *American Sociological Review,* 1961, *26,* 854–866.

Steiner, George A. *Top Management Planning.* London: Macmillan Company, 1969.

Chapter Three

CONTROL

TYPES OF CONTROL
Directing or Correcting
Individual, Group, or Organizational
THE CONTROL PROCESS
RECIPROCITY OF CONTROL
REACTION TO CONTROL
ACHIEVING CONTROL

Ackoff (1970) describes control as the evaluation of implemented decisions, including decisions to do nothing. Dalton (1971) argues that control implies that (1) there is some standard or set of standards; (2) performance is compared to the standards, either on a discrete or a continuous basis; and (3) as a result of this comparison, corrective action is taken. Is there control if corrective action is not required? If one can show that without the standards and comparisons some other performance would result, then control has been demonstrated. However, such a demonstration may be difficult to achieve without allowing the system to go out of control. Newman (1975) describes control as a pervasive and positive force that is effective only when it guides behavior. Though the term *force* may connote an ability to influence, *energy potential* may better express the tentativeness of controls being actualized. Control, as Newman describes it, relates to all kinds of endeavors and to be successful must be future oriented and dynamic. Ackoff, Dalton, and Newman all express the idea that control requires some standard of comparison and some action in regard to that standard.

Control and control mechanisms can be found almost everywhere; a thermostat is a simple control mechanism, for example. However, we are interested here in control that affects and is affected by managers. This type of a control is not of much value if it does not result in individuals behaving in the desired fashion, so controls, therefore, must address this issue. Performance standards will probably be used to describe the desired behavior. Actual behavior can then be compared to the performance standard, and some action in regard to that comparison can be taken. (If a standard does not exist, any performance is good performance.) The action taken may result in reward or a punishment, such as giving someone a raise, or firing, transferring, or not promoting a person. The key point is that control requires comparing behavior to a standard and then taking some action based on the comparison. Given the components of a management control system, control occurs as an ongoing process that supports performance, which is defined by the attributes measured of the specific outputs assessed.

TYPES OF CONTROL

This section will discuss five typologies of control, which represent the concepts of Newman (1975), Amey (1979), Koontz and Bradspies (1972), Dalton (1971), and Hopwood (1974). The typologies of Newman, Amey, and Koontz and Bradspies primarily address the nature of the information feedback used for regulation, what Ansari (1977) would call structural models of control. Dalton and Hopwood, on the other hand, are more concerned with the behavior of individuals; such models Ansari would categorize as behavioral approaches to control.

Directing or correcting

Newman (1975) identifies three types of control: steering, yes-no, and postaction. Steering controls are forward looking, attempting to adjust the process before it is complete. Implementation of a capital budget is an example of steering control. The rate and types of investment are altered over time in order to achieve the desired goal. Yes-no controls are screening controls, much like quality control on a manufacturing line. The element of interest is either accepted or rejected. Newman offers the example of the border guard allowing a car either to pass or not to pass. Postaction controls occur after the act is completed, when results are compared to a standard. Postaction controls thus represent report card information, useful for determining rewards and providing planning input. Newman uses budgetary control as an example. Financial budgets, though often serving as major control devices, are not necessarily the best controls. Financial budgets tend to emphasize input, which may or may not relate to the output of the organization. Moreover, the dollar measures may be too gross to elucidate specific problems. Also, budgets normally have a very short time frame and limited scope (Newman, 1975). Budgets can be used for other than postaction control, as will be shown later in the chapter.

The same information may be used for different types of control by different individuals. For instance, assume that for a college course the due dates for term papers are staggered. The grades on the first papers turned in represent postaction control for the writers of those papers because those grades occur after the fact. However, for the students who have not yet submitted papers, the grades on the first papers can be used for steering control, guiding their paper-writing behavior. As another example, assume a department head makes a decision regarding the presentation of the annual budget and after the presentation receives negative criticism from higher management. For that particular department head the criticism represents postaction control. However, for the other department heads, the criticism represents steering control—if they have not yet presented their budgets.

Steering, yes-no, and postaction controls focus on different behaviors or elements of the process of interest. Steering controls provide direction on how to drive from point A to point B to point C. Yes-no controls presume the appropriate route is taken from A to B to C, and measure only whether the car went through the checkpoints on time along the way. The driver may have gone cross-country through the fields between checkpoints. Postaction control does not ask whether the driver went through points A and B to get to C but is concerned only with whether the driver got to point C. One can argue that postaction control gives more freedom to the operator of the process. The more the controller moves the control system toward postaction controls and away from steering controls, the less the controller can do to change or guide the process. If a one-time process is controlled by postaction controls, everyone will have to wait until the process is completed to find out if it worked or not. If steering control is used, a better estimate of whether the process will work may be available. On the other hand, controlling some kind of repetitive process using postaction control allows for changes in future products. Whether a type of control is restrictive or not depends to a large extent on the situation and individuals involved in that situation.

Amey (1979) makes essentially the same distinctions as Newman, except that Amey uses a feedback model common in engineering disciplines to describe the types of control. The forward-looking steering control that Newman describes is a learning model in Amey's context. The learning framework means that there is a pattern recognizer to help insure that optimal or near optimal decisions are made. Newman's yes-no control corresponds to Amey's adapter, which establishes variability and can be used for feedback for new elements coming through the system. Finally, postaction control in Amey's terminology becomes the compensator, an after-the-fact control.

Koontz and Bradspies (1972) divide control into feedforward and feedback controls. Feedforward control aims at meeting the problem of delay in feedback by monitoring inputs and predicting the effects on outcome variables. Feedback control, on the other hand, is after-the-fact evaluation. Though much has been said about feedforward control, its characteristics are very much the same as Newman's steering control or Amey's learning control. This text will not use the division of controls into feedback and feedforward. However, the reader should be aware of the distinction, since it is used by some writers. Table 3.1 presents the three categorizations of control.

Table 3.1 Three Categorizations of Control

Newman	Amey	Koontz and Bradspies
Steering	Learning model	Feedforward
Yes–No	Adapter	—
Postaction	Compensator	Feedback

Individual, group, or organizational

Dalton (1971), and Hopwood (1974) look at controls using a slightly different approach. Dalton describes controls as being of three types: (1) organizational, which tend to deal with very formal, structured dimensions; (2) individual or self, which tend to be much less structured; and (3) informal, which to a large extent fall between organizational and individual controls in terms of structure and individuals involved. Table 3.2 shows the types of controls, who administers them, and relevant factors relating to each type. In the Dalton model, characteristics that distinguish each type of control include the source of the directions for the controls, behavioral and performance measures used for control, signals that indicate corrective action is necessary, reinforcements or rewards for compliance, and sanctions for noncompliance.

Hopwood, using a similar typology, demonstrates how administrative, social, and self controls affect control of the enterprise. The administrative, social, and self controls correspond very closely to Dalton's organizational, group, and individual controls. Figure 3.1, as presented by Hopwood, depicts the fact that controls of an enterprise are influenced by other control systems. The differences in the type of controls are not important in themselves. Their importance lies in the fact that in any situation in which there is control, that control can exist along multiple dimensions. Table 3.3 portrays these multiple dimensions by putting the typologies of Dalton and Hopwood on the horizontal axis and those of Newman and Amey along the vertical axis. Table 3.3 demonstrates that it may not be enough merely to know whether the control system is postaction, yes-no, or steering or whether it is administered individually, socially, or organizationally. To understand the influence of a particular control within an organization, one must identify the unique combination of control characteristics and situational contingencies.

THE CONTROL PROCESS

Some process must be available for designing controls compatible with the goals, design, and objectives of the organization. Management must be involved in their design; it is not a job for the techni-

Table 3.2 Types of Control in Organizations

Controls Administered By	Direction for Controls Deriving From	Behavioral and Performance Measures	Signal for Corrective Action	Reinforcements or Rewards for Compliance	Sanctions or Punishments for Noncompliance
Organization	Organizational plans, strategies, responses to competitive demands	Budgets, standard costs, sales targets	Variance	Management commendation → Monetary incentives, promotions	Request for explanation → Dismissal
Informal group	Mutual commitments, group ideals	Group norms	Deviance	Peer approval, membership, leadership	Kidding → Ostracism, hostility
Individual	Individual goals, aspirations	Self-expectations, intermediate targets	Perceived impending failure, missed targets	Satisfaction of "being in control" → Elation	Sense of disappointment → Feeling of failure

Source: G. W. Dalton, Motivation and control in organizations, in G. W. Dalton and P. R. Lawrence (Eds.), *Motivation and Control in Organizations* (Homewood, Ill.: Richard D. Irwin, 1971), p. 15.

Figure 3.1 Pattern of Organizational Control

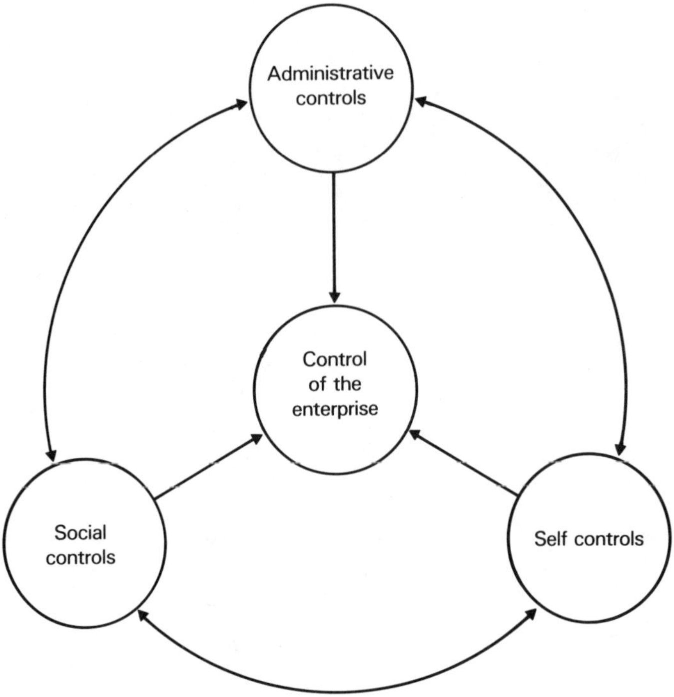

Source: A. Hopwood, *Accounting and Human Behavior* (Englewood Cliffs, N.J.: Prentice-Hall, 1974), p. 22.

cians only. To understand better how to design useful controls, this section discusses ideas presented by Newman (1975) and Ackoff (1970).

Newman (1975) presents control design as a series of six elements or steps. First, if controls are to work, desired results must be defined in measurable terms and linked to results attributable to specific individuals. However, such well-defined measures may not always be possible. That does not mean that a control system cannot be developed but simply that the system will not be as finely calibrated as desired. For instance, Demski (1976) demonstrates that measuring collective performance may foster desired patterns

Table 3.3 Examples of Control in Organizations

	Administrative or Organizational	Social or Informal Group	Individual
Learning or steering controls	Use of projections to determine potential budget variances	Advising a new employee of group norms	Setting short-term personal performance goals based on a desired professional position ten years hence
Pattern-recognizer or yes–no controls	Quarterly budget review to determine whether a project should continue	Not being invited to socialize after work with coworkers	Asking for a promotion after successfully negotiating a large contract
Compensatory or postaction controls	A bonus given to a manager for keeping within the previous year's budget	Kidding a colleague about having lunch with the boss too often	Leaving the organization after not being promoted

of behavior that is unachievable when individual performance is being measured. However, though group goals may be achieved, identifying a "free rider" may be difficult.

Effective control is largely based on predicted rather than actual results. The second step therefore, is for the designer to establish whether the predictors of results can be identified early in the process. This view argues for the use of steering controls to maintain the direction of purposeful behavior. Newman lists five predictors of results: measurements of inputs, success of early steps, monitoring of process variables, existence of symptomatic conditions, and relative deviation from assumed operating conditions. Each of these can be used to foretell results from the system.

Given the definition of desired results and a well-structured system for predicting them, the third step is to select composite feedback. Selecting composite feedback means selecting the predictors that are useful within the given system. Useful characteristics in a feedback scheme include:

1. *Promptness*—The information must be current to be useful. In this context, data are current if their age permits them to be used for the desired purpose.
2. *Reliability*—Prompt information that is unreliable is of little value. To be reliable, the information must describe the events consistently over time.
3. *Coverage*—Coverage refers to the degree to which the indicators give a comprehensive picture of the situation of interest. As Ridgway (1956) has pointed out, a single dimension can be a dangerous indicator; it may capture some but not all key elements of performance.
4. *Expense*—As in any accounting and control system, the economic value of the information should be greater than its cost.

The characteristic of validity could be added to the list. Validity deals with the degree to which the indicators are a true measure of the situation of interest. Coverage to some degree deals with the characteristic of validity. However, coverage emphasizes the completeness of the indicators, whereas validity emphasizes their quality.

As the fourth step it is necessary to set some par value or standard for each predictor or desired result. Though the end results are identified for the predictor, there still is no way of knowing whether that result is good or bad without a par value. Underestimating personnel needs by 10 percent on a specific job may be acceptable, but a 15 percent error may indicate that the estimating procedure needs to be reviewed. In other words, setting the par value means developing the control limits within which deviations are acceptable.

Once the initial four steps are accomplished, the flow of information must be specified: the fifth step. What, to whom, when, and how should the information be reported? The control information should be part of a formal reporting system.

Specification of the information flow is not a trivial effort. Let us look at the design of the information flow a little more closely before discussing the sixth step identified by Newman. Erroneous assumptions about information needs can facilitate the development of a poorly specified information flow. Ackoff (1970) lists five assumptions underlying the development of erroneous information systems.

The first erroneous assumption is that managers critically need more information. This assumes there is some model against which the information need can be compared. It is not at all clear that such a model exists. However, the voluminous output of information systems would indicate that the manager probably has an overabundance of irrelevant information. Therefore one of the major functions of the information system is to filter and condense information for the manager. However, to do this assumes some model of the decision maker's processes exists. Although such a model may not exist, questioning the relevance of the information prior to generating more of it does at least focus attention on the information-generating effort.

That managers need the information they want and know what information they need is the second erroneous assumption. Like the first, the justification for this assumption is not at all obvious. As Ackoff argues, it has long been known in science that the less a phenomenon is understood, the more variables and information that are required to explain it. Analogously, the less a manager understands a particular decision to be made, the more information the manager will request. To specify the information the manager needs, some model of the decision to be made must be developed.

The third erroneous assumption is that by giving the manager the information that is needed, the manager's decisions will then improve. However, if we know what information is necessary to make the decision, we do not need a decision maker to do it. The decision is programmable. If we are not sure precisely how to solve the problem, more information is not necessarily going to help. The required information to solve the problem likewise will not help if we do not know how to use it. Analyses of the first assumption (more is better) and this assumption are complementary. The analysis of the first assumption identifies the focus of the search—relevance to the decision maker—and the analysis of the third assumption identifies the point at which the search is completed.

Assumption four is that more communication means better performance. To quote Ackoff, "When organizational units have inappropriate measures of performance that put them into conflict with each other, as is more often the case than not, communication between them may hurt overall performance, not help it" (1970, p. 119).

The fifth and last assumption is that a manager does not need to know how information in an information system is developed but only how to make the information available. But the manager who does not understand the process that generates the information will not be able to evaluate the information coming from the system. And the manager who cannot evaluate the information will be left essentially with the decision of whether to trust the information—a decision based on faith, superstition, personal bias, or experience.

The analyses of the five assumptions indicate that, just as the control system relates to the organization, the information system accompanying the control system must relate to the design of the overall control system and the organization. The information system must be compatible with the goals, objectives, and measurements of those goals and objectives as contained in the control system. Management must be involved in the design of the information system. Its design is not a job for the technicians only.

Now we return to Newman's (1975) sixth and final step in control design, which is to evaluate and take corrective action. To take the corrective action, a series of tasks must be completed. If the control system indicates a potential area of concern, the predictors used must be confirmed and elaborated on. Confirmation may entail double-checking the data source or making the measurements a second time. Elaborating on the predictors may mean seeking information that complements the original predictor in order to obtain a more comprehensive picture of the situation of interest. The predictor may not only indicate problems directly related to its original purpose but may also portend effects in other areas. In the latter case the corrective action taken could be multidimensional depending on the complexity of the system. The action also will probably be unique, in that the particular situation may never recur. Moreover, not all the possible alternatives will be predetermined. All these considerations indicate that the response to the deviation is probably not programmable. In some cases replanning may be the reaction to the deviation. The correction process could be iterative: finding that the correction does not work can improve the correction process, which in turn will indicate corrections to be made to the work process.

A slightly different view from Newman (1975) of the same steps or process is given by Ackoff (1970), who describes a four-step process:

1. Predict the outcomes of decisions in the form of performance measures.
2. Collect information pertaining to actual performance.
3. Compare actual performance with the predicted performance.
4. When a decision is shown to have been deficient, correct the process or procedure that produced the decision and as much as possible correct the results of that decision.

In essence these points refer to the same process that Newman characterized as prediction, collection, comparison, and correction.

Newman's and Ackoff's steps for design indicate the complexity of the considerations necessary for control systems. However, the specificity with which each dimension of the control system criteria can be stated varies and in general is vague. For instance, though one can say that the objectives should be measurable for planning and control purposes in a specific situation, there is no clear rule to say what is a measurable objective and what is not a measurable objective.

RECIPROCITY OF CONTROL

Individuals can only be controlled inasmuch as they accept the control. It may appear in a given situation that there is perfect control. However, the individuals involved may simply be feeding the system faulty information and doing something contrary to the approved behavior. On the other hand, if there is reciprocity of control, both sides are probably getting what they want and are being controlled through mutual reinforcement.

A student of mine tells an anecdote about a controller and a personnel officer that illustrates how reciprocity of control operates. In a particular government installation a new civilian personnel officer had joined the staff. The controller had been there for years. The new personnel officer had a higher government rating than the controller. Previously, whenever the controller wanted to move someone, change position descriptions, or hire somebody, he would send a request to the personnel office to justify the changes, and the changes would be approved. Soon after the personnel officer arrived, the controller submitted a request for a new position. The personnel officer sent the controller's request back, indicating there was no justification for the position. The personnel officer's control system consisted of a manual that identified a controller's office as having just so many people doing various jobs. According to the manual the controller's office did not qualify for the position. The personnel officer, because of his high job level, had been in the habit of signing and submitting a time card weekly and not clocking in daily. The controller, apparently angered by the refusal of a new position, told the personnel officer to clock in every day. The personnel officer, fairly high up in government service, had probably not punched a time card for fifteen years. He complained to the individual in charge of the government installation, who pointed out that the regulations required that an employee sign in or punch in daily, so the personnel officer complied. Then about a month later the controller resubmitted the request for the additional position, and it was approved. The personnel officer did not punch in after the approval. So everybody was happy. It should be noted, though, that the personnel officer and the controller achieved their goals by implicitly agreeing to subvert the official control system, not by complying with it.

In order for a control system to work, both sides have to agree to it and cooperate. If the individuals participating do not cooperate, there will not be any control. It is that simple. Designing a system that the individual controlled will accept is probably the key factor in the design process.

REACTION TO CONTROL

The goal of control is to help the organization adapt to its changing environments. However, this goal is not always achieved. Merton (1940), Gouldner (1954), and Selznick (1949) have studied the way people react to control systems in organizations. These three models have been discussed and related by Ashton (1976) and Dalton (1971). Briefly, what the Gouldner, Merton, and Selznick models demonstrate is that there are unintended and sometimes pathological consequences of control. Control is a paradox.

Merton (1940) observed that as an organization grows larger and larger, management attempts to insure reliability as a means to guarantee control over the organization's process. To develop this reliability, rules are instituted that prescribe, in an impersonal manner, specific behaviors. As the rules become more prominent as a means to administer rewards and punishments, the rules become objectives in themselves. The rules of the organization become internalized and valued as ends in themselves, and their original purpose tends to be ignored or forgotten. For instance, these rules may govern interactions with customers or clients: "Sorry, store policy is that exchanges are made only if you have the receipt. You lost the receipt; therefore, an exchange is not possible—even though the garment has our label on it." The members of the organization begin to behave rigidly if the needs in the environment cannot be met within the categories described by the rules: "It does not matter that the garment is defective—you must have the receipt." The members of the organization conclude that there is obviously something wrong with the needs in the environment: "I'm sorry about not being able to exchange the garment. Next time remember to put your receipt in a safe place." This lack of response to the environment prompts the institution of more rules to insure a more reliable response to the needs in the environment, which in turn create more specific categories into which the behavior must fit, which in turn produce more problems in responding to a changing environment, which in turn generate more rules.

Gouldner (1954) also addresses management's desire to control the organization by emphasizing the impersonal rules that specify acceptable behavior. The rules are supposed to provide a means for individuals to know what needs to be done and how to accomplish it appropriately. If the system goes according to plan, the interaction between supervisor and worker is limited by rules to specific instances. Formalizing interaction in this way is supposed to reduce interpersonal tension among the members of the organization. However, the same rules that serve to limit supervisory control also specify minimum acceptable behavior. The supervisor then tries to raise productivity above the acceptable minimum. This interaction tends to generate greater tension between the individuals, and the result is more rules are devised that even more precisely specify minimal acceptable behavior.

Selznick (1949) emphasizes management's need or desire to delegate authority. The delegation of authority is supposed to lead to a more specialized focus of effort, which in turn increases the ability to deal with complex problems, albeit in a limited area. However, the increased specialization creates a potential for myopia by encouraging employees to internalize the goals reflected by the specialized subunit. If there is interaction between the departments, a sense of competition can grow, causing conflicts and inattention to the organization's overall objectives and goals.

The three models of Merton, Gouldner, and Selznick differ in design and emphasis, but each identifies unintended consequences of control arising from compliance with the system and resistance to change external to the system. As discussed in Chapter One, the unintended consequences of control systems are due to some degree to the inability of the designer to specify fully the desired behaviors. Chapters Five and Six analyze why it is difficult if not impossible to fully specify the desired behaviors.

Newman (1975) argues that a well-developed control system permits management by exception. His argument may be tautological, in that a well-developed control system defines a system without any major problems. However, if the control system emphasizes punishment and negative reinforcement or has not clearly identified appropriate behaviors, undesirable results can occur. For instance, management by exception operationally defines success as avoiding behavior that has been identified as problematic. If such behaviors are exhibited, supervisory intervention will result. Though the intervention may not be a punishment in and of itself, it does imply that the manager is not able to control the operation in a suitable manner. If the tolerances and behaviors are well specified, resources will probably be allocated for the purpose of insuring that all behavior is within acceptable tolerances (Kerr, 1975). As long as the tolerances and behaviors accurately capture performance, the system should work. However, if they are less than perfect measures of performance, unmeasured aspects of performance may be ignored. This point is illustrated by a conversation I heard between the head of a local service department and a visitor from a higher level in the organization:

> *Local department manager:* "I understand why you're out here, and I know what you must do, but just picking that dimension and saying that represents my department's performance just isn't realistic because we do so many other things."
>
> *Visitor:* "Yes, but we can't identify and we can't measure those other factors. I've got direction from the director that we are going to come up with performance measures for every department."

The visitor was insisting that numerical measures of performance would be developed. Those numbers, when developed, would be watched both by the local managers and by the administrators at the upper levels of the organization. The local employees would make every effort to insure that those numbers were acceptable. Would those measures capture performance? Probably not. If the situation involved a personnel department and the measure of performance were the number of people hired or number of days a job was left empty, jobs could get filled very quickly with people who on paper met minimum qualifications. However, that would not necessarily mean that the most qualified people available had been placed in the jobs.

One of my students gave a similar example. He pointed out that in the Navy one of the factors for measuring a commanding officer's performance was the reenlistment rate among those in his command. The rate was calculated as a percentage of the number of people considered eligible for reenlistment. On my student's ship the rate was very low. In an effort to improve the situation, one of the ship's staff consulted the staff on a ship that always had a very high reenlistment rate. On this ship anyone not planning to reenlist was marked ineligible for reenlistment. Consequently, the ship had a 100 percent reenlistment rate about half of the time and about a 90 percent rate the rest of the time. This was how the staff on the successful ship had responded to the performance measure.

Using just one measure of performance invites such practices. Ridgway (1956) points out that one solution to the problem is to use a second measure that balances the first. For the previous example assume that the commanding officer also had to report the number of people who were not recommended for reenlistment. This second measure would balance the first one, and maximizing a particular measure of performance would become less advantageous. A sufficient number of diverse measures make it more difficult to subvert the system. However, as Ridgway points out, if there are many measures, the people being evaluated may throw up their hands and say, "I do not know what to do. If I do this, I fall behind over here and if I do that, I fall behind over there. I think I'll try and play it safe and do as little as possible." A more positive approach would be to present the measures as an integrated set relating to specific goals. However, if the interrelated set does not fully capture performance, the unmeasured dimensions may still be ignored. The topics of what to measure and how to measure are discussed more thoroughly in Chapters Four and Five.

Another reason that control systems do not always work is because of overlapping spheres of influence (Dalton, 1971). If two individuals are attempting to accomplish some task and must control the same activity in so doing, there is a potential for conflict and a breakdown of control. Or, as Milton Friedman (1962) has stated, the freedom for me to swing my fist is limited by the proximity of your chin; I have only limited control over the resources that are supposedly mine to use.

ACHIEVING CONTROL

Making the system work means putting together the structure, the people, and the tasks in a way that is compatible. Factors identified (Anthony and Herzlinger, 1980; Lawler and Rhode, 1976; Newman, 1975) as potentially inhibiting compatibility include:

1. Using easily measured factors in the control system. An attribute of performance that is easily measured may not necessarily be useful or appropriate.
2. Focusing on short-run rather than long-run results. (See Rappaport (1981) and Hayes and Abernathy (1980) for a discussion of the infatuation with short-run results and its impact on American industry.)
3. Not allowing the control system to adapt to its changing environment.
4. Not using qualified people. It may seem a pious platitude, but the most important ingredient in any system is quality staff members.

Ways to promote compatibility and foster a positive system can also be identified (Newman, 1975):

1. Focus on what the desired impact on individuals is to be. Design the system for the desired action or reaction and maintain a focus on those actions or reactions.
2. Match the kind of control system with the desired results. If a learning or steering control is called for, do not design compensatory or postaction controls.
3. Limit control system pressure.
   a. Set the performance level at "normal." Although this practice may lead to all of the problems identified in the previous section in the Gouldner model, it represents a positive guideline because it asks for realistic performance from the workers. However, identifying realistic performance does not guarantee that the "minimum behavior syndrome" will be prevented.
   b. Allow individual flexibility to get the job done and be concerned about output. If using steering controls, insure that they explicitly recognize equifinality.
   c. Foster an attitude of accepting and expecting good performance from the staff. Once again, this factor underscores that it is the participants who make the system work.

4. Select a so-called total system with extreme caution. No system will be complete; therefore, a close inspection of both the explicit and implicit weaknesses of any system is necessary.
5. Emphasize that the control units are service and resource units designed to aid the line or production units. Auditors can help solve problems, not just find problems, and controllers can facilitate budget preparations and expenditures.
6. Place control activities close to the operations. While this increases the probability of the controller being coopted, if there is a professional attitude among staff, the proximity to the control group will help to reduce and resolve problems more quickly. Feedback will be fast; local facts can be evaluated quickly. The information may be prompt enough for steering or learning control if desired.
7. Have generalists balance the controls. As emphasized more than once in this book, the design of controls should not be left to technicians, whether they are accountants, computer systems experts, or engineers.

Finally, think again about reciprocity of control. Is it possible to control without being controlled (Dalton, 1971)? Is the dog walking the person or is the person walking the dog? Does it matter?

SUGGESTED READINGS

Amey, Lloyd R. *Budget Planning and Control Systems.* London: Pitman Publishing, 1979.

Ashton, Robert H. Deviation-amplifying feedback and unintended consequences of management accounting systems. *Accounting, Organizations and Society,* 1976, *1*(4), 289–300.

Blau, Peter M. *Bureaucracy in Modern Society.* New York: Random House, 1956.

Newman, William H. *Constructive Control: Design and Use of Control Systems.* Englewood Cliffs, N.J.: Prentice-Hall, 1975.

Ridgway, V. F. Dysfunctional consequences of performance measurement. *Administrative Science Quarterly,* September 1956, 240–247.

Skinner, B. F. *Reflections on Behaviorism and Society.* Englewood Cliffs, N.J.: Prentice-Hall, 1978.

Chapter Four

EVALUATION

EVALUATION DEFINED
The Measurement Definition
The Congruence Definition
The Judgment Definition
TYPES OF EVALUATION
What to Evaluate
  Effort
  Effectiveness
  Adequacy
  Efficiency
  Process
When to Evaluate
  Context Evaluation
  Input Evaluation
  Process Evaluation
  Product Evaluation
Levels or Types of Evaluation

PURPOSES OF EVALUATION
EVALUATIONS NOT WORTH DOING
EVALUATIONS—INSIDE OR OUTSIDE
ACCOUNTANTS AS EVALUATORS
EVALUATION AND CONTROL
SUMMARY

This chapter discusses evaluation and the evaluation process. This topic is included because, as discussed in Chapter One, the information required for management control is often part of an evaluation system. Therefore understanding how evaluation systems operate and affect the organization is relevant to the analysis and design of management control systems. This chapter also introduces the issues of what to measure, how to measure, and how the measures relate to the goals of the organization. These measurement topics are covered in greater depth in Chapter Five.

EVALUATION DEFINED

What is evaluation? In Chapter One evaluation was described as the process used to analyze the relationship between actual and desired effects. However, the description does not define what constitutes the analysis. Stufflebeam et al. (1971) identifies three accepted definitions of what constitutes evaluation: measurement, congruence, and judgment. A discussion of each of these evaluation definitions follows.

The measurement definition

The measurement definition simply says that evaluation is identical to measurement and builds directly on attempts to measure psychological attributes or characteristics. This approach emphasizes the need to develop specific measurement instruments that can be used repeatedly in an objective fashion. Over time these instruments develop a high degree of reliability. The data can be manipulated mathematically and thus can be used to develop norms and standards for the particular operation of interest.

The problem with this approach is that it tends to make evaluation a very narrow, instrumental activity. It is concerned with measuring a particular attribute and not with the process that developed the attribute. That is, a particular attribute that cannot be measured with some type of instrument is considered unsuitable for evaluation and therefore unimportant. Additionally, the measurement definition tends to define an attribute in terms of the instrument used to measure it. For instance, intelligence may be defined as the score on an IQ test and profit as the bottom line on an income statement; but it is doubtful whether IQ or profit are the same as the particular attributes being measured. However, the cost and effort necessary to develop a particular kind of instrumentation may cause a resistance to developing new and different instruments. Moreover, the evaluation process becomes tied to the particular instrument and the rationale for making particular kinds of judgments becomes obscured.

The congruence definition

A second widely accepted definition identified by Stufflebeam et al. is that evaluation is the determination of the congruence between performance and objectives. Is the definition useful? It does suggest that evaluation depends on a clear statement of objectives and performance measures. The emphasis of the evaluation appears to be not on particular attributes of performance but on general objective performance. Moreover, the evaluation process appears to be well integrated with the actual transformation process of the organization. The measurement definition considers evaluation to be an after-the-fact measurement of some attribute. By contrast, the congruence definition, given the integration with the transformation process, presents the possibility for ongoing measurement of whether objectives are being met. The immediate feedback allows managers to adjust the process as the process occurs. Given that the evaluation is of the objectives relating to a particular process, evaluation information should be available then on both the process itself and the outputs of that process. This definition reinforces the view that evaluation is related to a particular process in general and not to some specific measurable attribute.

However, in order to make the congruence definition of evaluation work, some objectives have to be selected and measured. What objectives are selected? Usually short-term objectives. Why? Because the evaluator is looking for something that is quantifiable. Stufflebeam et al. (1971) argue that the evaluators pick specific measurable results because they want to be able to measure performance against a specific objective. The specific measurable results are probably short-term in nature. Though the results may suffer from the same problems prevalent with use of the measurement definition, measurable objectives are needed if the evaluation is to be conducted. If the objectives are not specified, there is no sense in conducting an evaluation.

Specific measurable objectives will probably not exist. Some long-run goal may exist, but it will not have been translated into short-term operational objectives that can be measured and used for evaluation purposes. For instance, it is safe to assume that the goal of most small businesses is to make a profit. However, many small businesses neither have a profit plan for the year (either formal or informal) nor do they actively manage their cash. To make the short-run evaluation, the evaluator will probably be forced to develop, or at least help the owners of the small business develop, specific measurable objectives.

As an example of implementing the congruence definition, Stufflebeam et al. discuss an education program whose stated goal is to educate people. Do current graduates of the program demonstrate that they have been educated? If it is a graduate program in management, performance of the graduates over a ten- to twenty-year period will probably answer that question. Performance ten to twenty years from now may help address the question of how useful is management education, but future performance is not going to help answer the question of immediate concern. The evaluator must then start looking for more proximate measures by asking questions such as: Do the students get good grades? Do the students work hard? Do they get good jobs on graduation? The evaluator asks questions that may not have anything to do with the occurrence of education, but their answers are measurable. Consider, for instance, the question of whether a particular course is required of the students. One can assume that the course may provide an environment for education to occur, but it certainly is not a necessary or a sufficient condition for education to occur.

It may be argued that for profit-oriented organizations the measure of organizational performance—profit—is simpler to identify. However, profit is ony an indicator of long-run wealth maximization. It would be difficult for an organization to have an economic profit on a continuing basis and not be contributing to its long-run wealth maximization. However, the profit figure that is used is an artifact of the accounting cycle, and it may not be a valid indicator of economic profit. In and of itself, profit might be treated as a relatively neutral output of the accounting cycle and balanced with other measures of performance. However, this is not always the case. As Hopwood (1974) has demonstrated, individuals exhibit at least three different managerial styles in the use of accounting information, profit data included: the budget-constrained style, the profit-constrained style, and the nonaccounting style. The *budget-constrained* manager is concerned that the budget be correct—year by year, quarter by quarter, and month by month. If performance is being measured by being on target, every effort will be made to ensure that the budget is on target. Individuals manipulate the budget information to make it look correct. The *profit-constrained* manager is interested in the impact of current decisions on longer-run profits, so the concern is with intermediate- to long-term results and is less with manipulating the accounting numbers. The *nonaccounting* style does not use accounting information to any major degree for evaluative purposes. Individuals do not manipulate the information because it is not used. Each manager receives the same information but uses it differently.

How are these distinctions relevant to the congruence definition and the question of profit as a good short-term measure of performance? If evaluations are made on the basis of being within budget—every six months or every year—the operation will probably be within budget. However, the longer run may be ignored.

Hopwood (1974) presents an anecdote about employees running capital investment items through expense accounts. The funds were not available for capital investments in the short run. By identifying capital investment items as expenses the budget for capital investment items was not exceeded. Although the numbers were within budget for the period, the results of the shifting may not have had anything to do with the true measurement of profit in the long term.

Profit-making organizations may have goals other than profit. One example is the Sycamore Ice Cream (SIC) Parlor in a small, tourist-oriented, Western community. SIC was run by two executives who opened it in their retirement years because they wanted something fun and productive to do. Their stated goal was to have the best old-fashioned ice cream parlor around. They wanted it to be like the parlors they remembered from their youth. To accomplish this, they did such things as furnish SIC with little round marble tables and wire-back chairs. They did make a profit, a very handsome one, but from an accounting standpoint they did not maximize profits. More tables could have been used. Product mix was not optimal: there was only ice cream and very select kinds of candy but no sandwiches or other fast foods. Moreover, ice cream cones were not sold. The customer had to go in and sit down for dish service. An analysis of SIC's operation indicated they could have made a greater profit by changing their strategy to include items such as ice cream cone sales. Then the ice cream parlor changed hands. Now ice cream cones were sold and sandwiches served. The parlor changed, and so apparently did the goals and measured profit.

What about the public image of a profit organization? How should it be measured and evaluated? Public image does relate to wealth maximization. (How can a firm achieve long-term wealth maximization when customers don't buy its products because the customers think it is destroying the environment?) Thus organizations spend a great deal on their images through public relations and corporate advertising. However, in the short term, these are discretionary expenses, not recouped in short-term profit.

The point is that short-term measurable objectives, for a profit-making and a nonprofit organization alike, are probably poor indicators of the organization's long-run goals. However, the congruence definition of evaluation does foster a need in the evaluator to find a short-term measure of performance. Additionally, the congruence definition tends to provide incentive to the evaluator to look for identifiable outputs or behaviors. These outputs or behaviors then become the ultimate criteria for every organizational action or decision and, as Fig. 1.1 indicated, come to be viewed as performance. Though the congruence definition does appear to have many advantages, the need to find measurable objectives creates problems that initially are not at all apparent.

The judgment definition

Stufflebeam et al. (1974) present a third definition of evaluation: professional judgment. This approach overcomes many of the weaknesses of the congruence and measurement definitions. First, the judgment definition is easy to implement. Second, it allows for evaluation of all attributes of an organization, quantifiable and nonquantifiable. Third, it provides for essentially an instantaneous evaluation because there is not a lengthy period to process the evaluation information through the evaluation machine. For instance, readiness inspections in the military are conducted by other professionals who are apparently aware of what military readiness is. Difficult issues such as promotion are often decided using a judgmental evaluation of performance. Why? Because the dimensions that need to be measured are often difficult to define and even more difficult to quantify. The judgmental evaluation is based on the very experience and expertise that are being evaluated.

The judgment definition is not without its problems, however. First of all, because the basis of the evaluation is an individual's professional judgment, the evaluation is unique to that individual. The reliability and objectivity of such evaluations can be questioned. Second, when judgmental evaluation is used, both the data being considered and the criteria by which the data are evaluated are ambiguous: those people being evaluated really do not know what is important and what is unimportant. Given these characteristics, normal analysis of the results of an evaluation is difficult, which in turn limits the generalizability of any judgment made. Finally, evaluation based on professional judgment is usually used because of ignorance of suitable measures of the underlying behaviors. As systems become better understood, evaluations typically move from judgmental ones to those based on more clearly stated measures and attributes. Table 4.1 summarizes the advantages and disadvantages accruing from each of the three definitions of evaluation.

Table 4.1 Advantages and Disadvantages Accruing from Different Definitions of Evaluation

	Advantages	*Disadvantages*
(1) Measurement	Builds directly on scientific measurement	Narrow instrumental focus
	Objective	Inflexible because of time and cost to produce new instruments
	Reliable	
	Data mathematically manipulatable	Obscures judgments and the criteria for making them
	Norms and standards emerge	
		Eliminates variables currently considered as not measurable or labels them unimportant
(2) Congruence	High degree of integration with the process.	Places evaluator in technical role
	Data available on process and structure	Focuses narrowly on objectives
	Possibility of feedback	Elevates behavior as the ultimate criterion of every action
	Objective referent and built-in criteria	
	Possibility of process as well as product data	Focuses on evaluation as a terminal process

(cont.)

Table 4.1 (cont.)

	Advantages	*Disadvantages*
(3) Judgment	Easy to implement	Dictated mainly because of ignorance or lack of sophistication
	Brings all variables into consideration	
	Takes experience and expertise into account	Questionable reliability
		Questionable objectivity
	Not time lag while waiting for data analysis	Not susceptible to ordinary scientific, prudential measures
		Both data and criteria are ambiguous
		Generalization very difficult

Source: Adapted from D. L. Stufflebeam, W. J. Foley, W. J. Gephart, E. G. Guba, R. L. Hammond, H. O. Merriman, and M. M. Provus, *Educational Evaluation and Decision Making* (Itasca, Ill.: F. E. Peacock Publishers, 1971), p. 15.

TYPES OF EVALUATION

Within any of the three definitions of evaluation and their subsequent approaches to the evaluation process, types or domains of evaluation can be identified. This section discusses two typologies of evaluation, those of Suchman (1967) and Stufflebeam et al. (1971).

What to evaluate

Suchman (1967) describes five types or levels of evaluation: effort, effectiveness, adequacy, efficiency, and process. Each is discussed in greater detail in this section. Attkisson and Broskowski (1978) present a table that summarizes the five levels (Table 4.2). As Suchman points out, the use of each evaluation level assumes that the level relates to the goals or objectives of the organization or operation being evaluated. However, as will be discussed presently, the validity of that assumption is questionable.

Table 4.2 Evaluative Domains: Typical Criteria and Measurement Tools

Evaluative Domains (see Suchman, 1967)	Typical Criteria and Informational Requirements	Typical Methodological Tools, Procedures, and Indices
I. Effort (Input)	Information about the amount and distribution of resources put into the program: • Sources of income and expenditures • Allocation of staff time • Numbers and types of clients • How dollars, staff, and clients are interrelated	• Management information systems • Explicit structural and process standards mandated by law, regulations, and accreditation bodies • Quality assurance procedures such as utilization review and peer review • Capacity for effort as reflected by indices of service availability, accessibility, comprehensiveness, and integration
II. Effectiveness (Output)	Information about the outcomes and effectiveness of program effort: • Clients' acceptance of services offered • Improvement in clients' status • Changes in incidence or prevalence of problems addressed by programs • Acceptability of services to clients • Effective linkage of clients to other necessary and appropriate service resources	• Scales measuring client functioning and status • Scales assessing client satisfaction • Goal-oriented idiosyncratic scales developed for specific clients • Rates of successful referrals for multi-problem clients • Range of services available that are known to be necessary for specific communities

Source: Adapted from C. C. Attkisson and A. Broskowski, "Evaluation and the Emerging Service Concept," in C. C. Attkisson, W. A. Hargreaves, M. J. Horowitz, and J. E. Sorenson (Eds.), *Evaluation of Human Service Programs* (New York: Academic Press, 1978), pp. 6–7.

(cont.)

Table 4.2 (cont.)

Evaluative Domains (see Suchman, 1967)	Typical Criteria and Informational Requirements	Typical Methodological Tools, Procedures, and Indices
	• Level of service availability and accessibility achieved over time	• Enumeration of cultural, linguistic, psychological, geographic, and organizational barriers to service accessibility; measurement of reduction in barriers to accessibility over time
III. Adequacy (Output ÷ Need)	Information about effort and performance relative to measures of community need or demand: • Match between efforts and needs • Adequacy of performance effectiveness relative to level of need • Appropriateness of clients being served relative to high-risk groups or mandated target populations • Awareness of services among citizenry	• Review and analyze mandated services or documented needs • Undertake needs-resources assessment methods • Review and analyze management information system and outcome assessment data to assess client utilization rates relative to known service needs, mandated target populations, and high-risk groups • Survey citizens' awareness of available services
IV. Efficiency (Output ÷ Input)	Information about how effort is organized so as to get greatest *performance* and *adequacy*: • Cost of providing effective services	• Calculation of costs per unit of service • Cost-outcome and cost-effectiveness comparisons using management information system data and outcome assessment data

		• Cost-effort-outcome-effectiveness comparisons for different target groups
• Efficiency studies to compare different organizational methods in costs and effectiveness
	• Comparisons of the efficiency and efficacy of different programs or methods of service	
V. Process (Outcome = Function of effort)	Information about the underlying processes by which effort is translated into outcome: • Specification of salient attributes, recipient characteristics, contextual conditions, and the potency and range of effects associated with the program • Identification of causal relations between effort and outcome • Establish maximal generalizability of effects to other environments • Control or explain other factors, independent of program effort, that could possibly account for program outcomes	• Descriptive, correlational, and experimental methodologies that vary type or amount of independent variables and measures immediate and long-range dependent variables
• Alternative quasi-experimental research designs
• Replication of studies demonstrating causal relationships
• Studies designed to establish and enhance data reliability and validity
• Decision-theoretic approaches to maximizing the quality of administrative decisions and thereby program efforts and outcomes
• Operations research methodologies
• Multisite, collaborative, randomized clinical trials

Effort. Effort is equivalent to input. Effort evaluation is measuring input values as indicators of meeting objectives. How many dollars were spent? How many patient days were there? How many beds are there in the hospital? All these are input measures of providing health care, but not necessarily good health care. The spending of dollars or the placing of beds in a room may be required for but does not guarantee good health care. How many steaming hours did a given ship log? Are steaming hours a measure of military preparedness? For the boiler tenders aboard the ship, however, steaming hours are an output measure because the end result of the boiler tender's job is making the ship go.

Examples of the tenuous relationship between effort measures and objectives of the organization are numerous and have been around for a long time. For instance, Blau (1956) presents the example of an employment service, where performance was evaluated by the number of individuals counseled. The personnel counseled a large number of people. However, the counselors made little effort to find jobs for those individuals. Apparently the agency's attitude was not to worry about getting the clients jobs because what was being measured was whether the clients were being counseled, not whether they found work. The use of input or resources may or may not mean that the job is being done.

Effectiveness. If inputs are too far removed from the meeting of organizational objectives, why not look at outputs? It would seem obvious that evaluating outputs—such as the number of units of production or the number of clients placed in jobs—would eliminate the problems of the input measures. Measuring outputs has many advantages. However, effectiveness is an arbitrary definition. Any number of widgets produced or people placed in jobs is output. Each level is as good as any other if output is looked at in general. To overcome this obvious deficiency in using the output measure by itself, Suchman suggests using the adequacy or impact measure.

Adequacy. Adequacy or impact looks at performance in terms of its larger environment. In other words, it is an output-to-need relationship. If the need and the output can be clearly identified, adequacy is a useful measure. However, what is the need for health services? What is the need for a specific product? The problem in any impact or adequacy level of evaluation is in identifying the global need.

Efficiency. The most familiar level of evaluation is probably efficiency, which in some ways overcomes the shortcomings of the previous levels. Efficiency relates output to input. In terms of efficiency, it is better if more can be done with the same amount of input or the same output can be generated with less input. Efficiency measures are useful for comparing the same process at two points in time or two different processes with the same output. However, like effort, effectiveness, and adequacy, the efficiency measure fails to identify how the output relates to the goal. Efficiency simply compares outputs with inputs.

Process. The final level of Suchman's model, the process measure, treats output as a function of input. It differs from a simple input measure because it focuses on the mechanism by which effort is translated into output. The function assumes an understanding of how the organization operates and an ability to predict what the output of the organization will be for a particular input.

In one sense, process evaluation is the highest level of evaluation. It allows a manager to view the entire transformation, starting with raw input and ending with the output necessary for meeting organizational goals. A well-understood and mechanized process such as a refinery can be viewed in this fashion. The problem with this level of evaluation is that few processes are understood well enough to be measured for evaluation purposes. How does the research manager know that a research scientist is going to produce suitable output? How does the salesperson know a particular presentation will produce a sale? If there is a problem measuring effort, effectiveness, efficiency, and impact and in making these indicators operational, then it will be difficult to overcome the complexities of specifying and measuring the process.

When to evaluate

Another view of the types of evaluation is given by Stufflebeam et al. (1971), who divide evaluation into context, input, process, and product categories. Stufflebeam et al. further relate the types of evaluation to specific kinds of decisions and divide decisions into four types: planning, structuring, implementing, and recycling. Planning decisions are used to determine goals and are essentially based on the diagnosis of a particular situation. Structuring decisions determine the project design resulting from questions and objectives generated during the planning decisions. Implementing decisions are made to control project operations. Finally, recycling decisions deal with reacting and making judgments in regard to project realignments and reallocations. Figure 4.1 depicts the rela-

Figure 4.1 An Evaluation Model

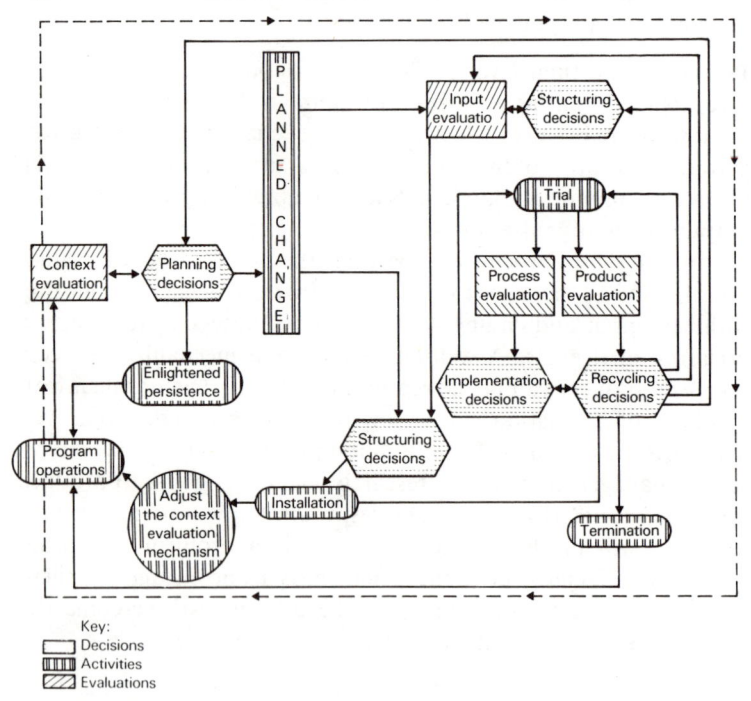

Source: Adapted from D. L. Stufflebeam, W. J. Foley, W. J. Gephart, E. G. Guba, R. L. Hammond, H. O. Merriman, and M. M. Provus, *Educational Evaluation and Decision Making* (Itasca, Ill.: F. E. Peacock Publishers, 1971), p. 236.

tionships between types of evaluation and kinds of decisions. In each case the evaluation is concerned with analyzing the relationship between the actual and desired effects of the decision.

Context evaluation. Context evaluation is used in determining the goals and objectives during the planning process and aids in diagnosing problems. Stufflebeam et al. (1971) distinguish two types of context evaluation: contingency and congruence. Contingency evaluation is used to look across the boundary of the system of interest and ask what-if kinds of questions. What if we do this? What if we try that? Where will this lead us? Congruency evaluation takes the environment and resource availability as given and then asks questions about how a particular goal or objective will be met. How do we work with what is available? How do we get to some acceptable alternative within the operation?

These two approaches to context evaluation can be compared further. As related to the discussion in Chapter One, the contingency evaluation is closely related to the goal-setting process, whereas congruent evaluation is more closely aligned with management control and the situational contingencies that influence the characteristics of the management control systems. Both contingency and congruence evaluation presume a data base. The contextual evaluation is a systematic macroanalytic approach, the results of which would be a suitable input for strategic or long-run planning.

Input evaluation. Once the goals are decided on, input evaluation must be accomplished. Input evaluation is useful in determining the structuring decisions for project designs. Input evaluation is concerned with the question of resource availability. How should the process be structured to utilize the resources? How is the information to be developed that will be helpful in structuring the process (for steering control or feedforward control)? Note the similarity between these ideas and those of Newman (1975) discussed in Chapter Three. The context and input evaluation discussed thus far take place prior to operationalizing the chosen alternative. The information is input for purposes of designing the process.

Process evaluation. Once the design is decided on, process evaluation is conducted. Process evaluation is used in implementing and controlling project operations. Analysis of the process as developed is made so that procedural problems can be identified and the process can then be altered. Additionally, process evaluation maintains a record of what is happening and sets the stage for the final step: product evaluation.

Product evaluation. Product evaluation focuses on output and is used in recycling decisions to judge and react to attainments. Product evaluation can be viewed as the decision to adjust the system in postaction control.

Levels or types of evaluation

Though the Stufflebeam et al. and the Suchman typologies have similarities, they approach evaluation from two different perspectives. Stufflebeam et al. (1971) are concerned with *when* to evaluate, and they view evaluation longitudinally, and as occurring at different stages. Suchman is concerned with *what* to evaluate at any moment in time: inputs, outputs, or combinations of the two. Suchman's levels of evaluation can be incorporated into each of the Stufflebeam et al. types of evaluation. Both views are also helpful in understanding the management control system as modeled in Fig. 1.1.

PURPOSES OF EVALUATION

Why are evaluations conducted? As Weiss (1972b) points out, many are carried out to generate information for guiding the future of a particular program. However, some evaluations are done for less than noble purposes: postponement, ducking responsibility, public relations, and fulfilling funding requirements. *Postponement* is a reason for conducting an evaluation when a decision maker seeks to delay a decision; Evaluating the required decision buys time. *Ducking responsibility* through evaluation occurs if either a manager or subordinate wishes to have information from an outside party, who can then be used as a scapegoat. Quite likely the decision maker already knows what the decision will be; the evaluation report is simply a way to shift responsibility. *Public relations* can generate an evaluation when the administrator of a program wants documentation showing that the program is useful and successful; the administrator may want to cover up specific problems with a cursory evaluation of the program or to evaluate only the strong parts of a weak program. Finally, the need for *fulfilling funding requirements* will often generate evaluations. Immediate superiors within organizations that require some kind of evaluation or operational audit in order to maintain funding support may order this kind of evaluation. Or the requirement may be generated by an external funding agency such as a governmental organization.

The use of evaluations for any of these four reasons defeats the purpose of evaluation. Evaluations, whether they be program audits, operational audits, or other types, are meant to be tools for gathering data for the future improvement of a program. Weiss (1972b) identifies six specific uses for an evaluation:

1. continuing or discontinuing a program;
2. improving practices and procedures of a program;
3. adding or dropping specific strategies and techniques within a program or operation;
4. instituting similar operations or programs elsewhere;
5. allocating resources among competing operations and programs;
6. accepting or rejecting a program approach or theory.

EVALUATIONS NOT WORTH DOING

Apart from evaluations conducted for inappropriate reasons, there are evaluations that are simply not worth doing (Weiss, 1972b). First, evaluations are useless when it is clear that the operation or program will continue as currently structured. If there is no question about whether the operation or program is going to exist as is, why bother evaluating? One argument is that the evaluation is required—but if there is no potential for change, why waste the resources doing the evaluation? Second, an operation or program should not be evaluated if it does not have a clear orientation. If you do not know where you are heading, one direction is as good as any other. With no clear orientation or objective to measure, there is nothing to evaluate. It does not matter if the evaluation focuses on outputs, inputs, process, or other characteristics. Third, an operation or program with competing objectives should not be evaluated. To conduct the evaluation the evaluator would have to arbitrate the objectives of the program with the individuals involved—not a function of evaluation. This is especially important in context evaluation, the function of which is to help identify objectives, not negotiate between factions. Fourth, the evaluation should not be done if there are not staff or dollars to conduct it appropriately. This may seem an obvious point, but evaluations are done on a shoestring budget, and then people wonder why the results are not very good. Why was the evaluation done? Because it was required. However, it is better not to do the evaluation in the first place, recognizing that it would have been a waste of time, effort, and resources.

EVALUATORS—INSIDE OR OUTSIDE

Evaluations conducted by outsiders presumably foster autonomy and objectivity. However, a symbiotic relationship may exist between the evaluator and the organization being evaluated. It can be argued, for example, that the audit staff of an accounting firm cannot evaluate critically the accounting systems of an organization if it was the management advisory staff of the same accounting firm that designed them. On the other hand, an evaluation conducted by insiders necessitates having an internal review, evaluation, or auditing section or committee. Is this really cost-effective, or would it be better to have an independent auditor or evaluator come in once a year? The internal audit group, depending on its quality, can facilitate the external audit. If the internal audit group does a good job and provides good documentation, the external auditors can to some extent evaluate the operation by rechecking the internal group's information and gathering additional data to verify the work of the internal group. If the internal group is doing substandard work, however, the external people have to come in and start from ground zero. Thus an internal group doing a good job serves a function and has the potential to save money for the organization.

ACCOUNTANTS AS EVALUATORS

How do accountants as accountants fit into the evaluation picture? Thomas (1976) discusses the issue of what kinds of evaluations are appropriate for accountants to conduct. He argues that accountants are obviously qualified to do traditional financial audits. They can also address the question of whether objectives set by other people are being met. However, in most cases accountants as accountants are not qualified to question whether the objectives are purposeful. The answer to that is probably political, or at least subjective, and not subject to analysis using traditional accounting techniques. The accountant as shareholder, employee, or voter, however, may evaluate such questions.

EVALUATION AND CONTROL

Does evaluation relate to control? Does knowing that an evaluation will occur influence a worker's behavior? Euske et al. (1980) present evidence that managers report greater satisfaction if they are being evaluated on items that put them in a favorable light rather than on items that they can control. Additionally, Hopwood (1974) has shown that evaluation data are manipulated to meet personal objectives. He presents a model (Fig. 4.2) demonstrating that the attributes measured, the goals of organizations, and the goals of individuals may have little in common. Individuals will look to fulfill organizational goals if the measured behaviors of the organization are in common with their own personal goals. If they are not, then the behaviors relating to personal goal achievement will take precedence, while the evaluation data is manipulated in order to insure organizational rewards.

Hopwood (1974) has demonstrated from the literature that if an attribute of a task is measured, employees pay attention to it be-

Figure 4.2 Measurement Reward Process with Imperfect Measurements

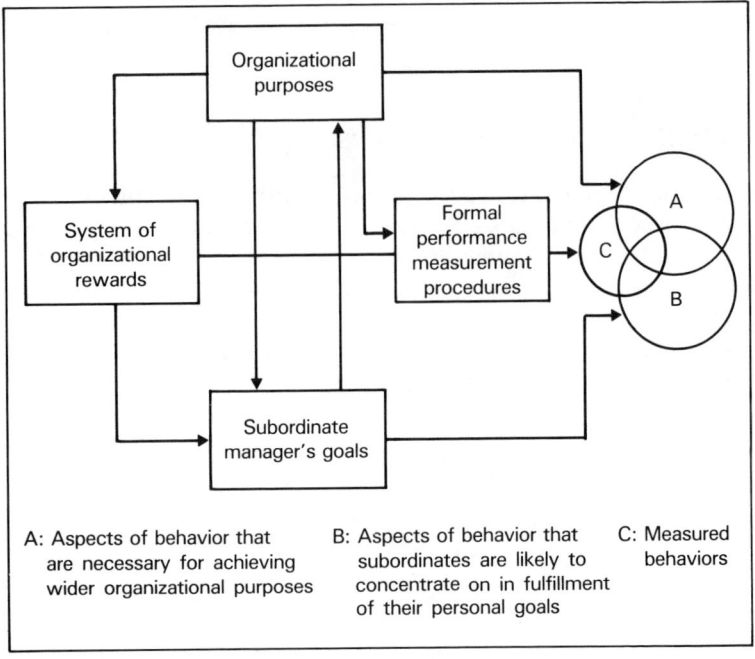

A: Aspects of behavior that are necessary for achieving wider organizational purposes

B: Aspects of behavior that subordinates are likely to concentrate on in fulfillment of their personal goals

C: Measured behaviors

Source: Adapted from A. Hopwood, *Accounting and Human Behavior* (Englewood Cliffs, N.J.: Prentice Hall, 1974), p. 108.

cause they apparently think the measures are going to be used for evaluation purposes. Employees want to make sure the measures "look right," so the measures influence employee behavior. For example, there was a case in which a manufacturing plant was pouring chromates directly into a river. The staff at corporate headquarters found out about this and told the plant manager to solve the problem. The plant manager said, "I can't fix it. If I install the equipment necessary to solve the problem, there will be an effect on my variances and profit. If that happens, I'll look bad." Though the corporate headquarters staff wanted to clean up the chromates, the act of doing so would have affected the measured performance of the plant manager, which was reported to that staff. As Rappaport (1981) argues, because managers are evaluated on three- to five-year measures of performance, their performance has a three- to five-year time frame.

The argument thus far has been that evaluation measures are short-run measures that do not necessarily relate directly to organizational goals. However, if the evaluations focused on long-run factors, managers would probably be at a loss, since evaluation is most useful when timely enough to be used for steering control. The manager can then adjust behavior to meet objectives.

SUMMARY

This chapter is intended to give the reader an appreciation for what evaluation is and what evaluation is meant to do. The chapter discussed definitions of evaluation, types of evaluation, uses for evaluation, and other related evaluation topics. Hopefully the reader detected that part of the discussion was missing. It was. The discussion took for granted that objects, objectives, inputs, and any other aspect or attribute of an operation can be measured for evaluative purposes. This, however, is not necessarily true. The issues of what to measure and how to measure it probably pose the largest stumbling blocks in the design and operation of any management control system. These two questions are the topic of the next chapter.

SUGGESTED READINGS

Attkisson, C. Clifford and Anthony Broskowski. Evaluation and the emerging human service concept. In C. Clifford Attkisson, William A. Hargreaves, Mardi J. Horowitz, and James E. Sorensen. *Evaluation of Human Service Programs*. New York: Academic Press, 1978, pp. 4–7.

Levitan, Sar A. and Gregory K. Wurzburg. *Evaluating Federal Social Programs: An Uncertain Art*. Kalamazoo; Mich.: Upjohn Institute for Employment Research, 1979.

Stufflebeam, Daniel L., Walter J. Foley, William J. Gephart, Egon G. Guba, Raymond L. Hammond, Howard O. Merriman, and Malcom M. Provus. *Educational Evaluation and Decision Making.* Itasca, Ill.: F. E. Peacock Publishers, 1971.

Suchman, Edward A. *Evaluative Research.* New York: Russell Sage Foundation, 1967.

Thomas, Arthur L. Evaluating the effectiveness of social programs. *Journal of Accountancy*, June 1976, pp. 65–71.

Weiss, Carol H. *Evaluation Research: Methods for Assessing Program Effectiveness.* Englewood Cliffs; N.J.: Prentice-Hall, 1972*b*.

Chapter Five

MEASUREMENT

ELEMENTS OF MEASUREMENT AND THE MEASUREMENT PROCESS
Scaling
   Nominal Scale
   Ordinal Scale
   Interval Scale
   Ratio Scale
Meaningfulness
Specification
Standards
Reliability
Validity
Types of Measurement
DEVELOPING MEASUREMENT SYSTEMS
FUNCTIONAL FIXATION
SUMMARY
SELECTED READINGS

Information is needed for carrying out all the functions discussed in previous chapters—planning, control, and evaluation. That information generally is in quantitative form and is the result of some measurement process. Though often taken for granted, the measurement process is central to the operation of an effective and efficient planning, control, or evaluation system. As discussed in Chapter One, apparently well-designed systems can produce undesired results because of a poor choice of the attributes measured. This chapter presents a general discussion of measurement, dealing first with selected elements of it, then covering the development of measurement systems, and finally discussing the phenomenon of functional fixation as it related to measurement.

In order to understand the issues involved in measurement, it is useful to discuss some of the basic concepts of theory development. Torgerson (1967) describes a theory as a set of constructs, concepts, or objects that are related to each other and to observable phenomena. A well-developed theory will contain a set of constructs or concepts that have formal, defined relationships and that are operationalized. Constructs are operationalized if there are rules of correspondence connecting the constructs to observable data. It is through these ties that a set of constructs comes to have empirical import. The set of constructs constitutes an analytical schema (Rudner, 1966). Thus to have a theory it is necessary to develop the rules of correspondence. If the constructs have operational definitions (that is, rules of correspondence), the analytical schema is empirically testable and can be classified as a theory. If there are no operational definitions of the constructs, the analytical schema is of no value for explaining phenomena. A more detailed discussion of the distinction between analytical schemata and theories is reserved for the following chapter. Figure 5.1 depicts the relationships among constructs, rules of correspondence, and observable data. (For more detailed consideration of the ideas presented here, see Margenau, 1950, chaps. 5 and 12.)

Key to the process of operationalizing the constructs is measurement, the assignment of numerals to attributes of objects according to rules. (Most authors would probably not differ vehemently with this wording as a general definition of measurement. See, for example, Stevens, 1946; Churchman, 1962; Torgerson, 1967. However, they probably would differ as to how those rules must be specified in order for measurement to occur. This point is discussed in greater detail later in the chapter.) It is important to note from this definition that the rules of correspondence relate to properties or attributes of objects, not to the objects

Figure 5.1 Example of a Well-Developed Theory

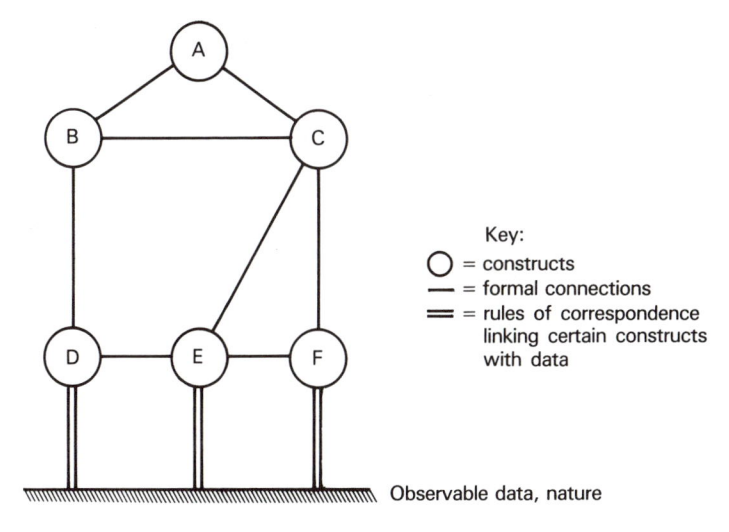

Key:
○ = constructs
— = formal connections
═ = rules of correspondence linking certain constructs with data

Observable data, nature

Source: Adapted from W. S. Torgerson, *Theory and Methods of Scaling* (New York: John Wiley & Sons, 1967), p. 3.

themselves. One can measure the size or weight of a chair, the chair's color, shape, or existence. It is not possible to measure "chairness" or "tableness." There is no measure of the essence of an object; the measures are of some extension of it. Similarly, people themselves are not measured; their height, color, shape, weight, or other characteristics are measured. Is performance measured? No, some attribute of performance is measured. Is satisfaction measured? No, some attribute of satisfaction is measured. The users of systems interact with the systems directly, but the information describing the system relates to attributes or an extension of the system and not to the system itself. Though interactions between a coworker and others demonstrate that the individual performs at a high level, the performance measures may be unacceptably low; that is, the individual may be allocating time and energy to overall maintenance of a system but not to the particular attributes of the system that are measured.

ELEMENTS OF MEASUREMENT AND THE MEASUREMENT PROCESS

Stevens (1946), Torgerson (1967), Churchman (1962), and Mock and Grove (1979) have identified and discussed various aspects of measurement and the measurement process. Their analyses are not necessarily complementary, but a discussion of some of the major concepts they have discussed is useful for understanding the influence of measurement and the measurement process on planning control and evaluation systems. Seven elements of measurement are discussed: scaling, meaningfulness, specification, standards, reliability, validity, and type.

Scaling

The types of scales relate to the characteristics of the real-number series that are used in a particular set of measurements (Torgerson, 1967). The characteristics are that (Torgerson, 1967, p. 15):

1. Numbers are ordered.
2. The difference between numbers are ordered. That is, the difference between any pair of numbers is greater than, equal to, or less than the difference between any other pair of numbers.
3. The series has a unique origin, indicated by the number 0. An important feature of this origin is that the difference between any pair of numbers containing 0 as the second member is the number of the other member. For example, the difference between the pair of numbers 7 and 0 is 7.

These three characteristics can be identified as order, distance, and origin.

The differences in measurement scales can be identified by the kinds of information found in the measurements. Does the measurement have order? Can differences be compared? Do the measurements have a unique origin? The differences in the scale types result from the fact that numerals can be assigned under different rules (Stevens, 1946). The scale types are differentiated on the basis of the kinds of empirical operations that may be legitimately performed on the numbers. The four traditional scales of measurements discussed are nominal, ordinal, interval, and ratio.

Nominal scale. The nominal scale is used as a means to classify attributes. The numbers used in the scale are simply used as a means to label or identify whether membership in a particular category exists or not. Stevens (1947) considers the nominal scale to be a scale of measurement, while Torgerson (1967) does not. Torgerson's argument is that the nominal scale does not use any of the inherent characteristics of the real-number series; order, distance, and origin are arbitrary parameters. A nominal scale can be created with signs, letters, or other marks of distinction. Stevens recognizes that not all agree that classifying attributes is a form of measurement, but he argues, that whatever it is called, the classification of attributes is a process that is used and must be reckoned with. One example of the nominal scale is the jersey numbers used in athletic events. The numbers name the individuals. If everybody's number is changed and if everyone has a different number, switching the numbers has no effect on the information content of the original numbers assigned. People with high numbers could be given low numbers and those with low numbers given high numbers, and the scale will be maintained. Inventory part numbers are another example of a nominal scale.

The scales distinguish objects from one another only by means of naming. It is possible to have multiple objects within a group, such as classifying individuals according to sex. Regardless, the classifying is a naming. The characteristics of the nominal scale are summarized in Table 5.1. There are fewer statistics that can be used with the nominal scale than with the other scales. Many of the nonparametric statistics are not applicable because an ordering of the data is assumed in addition to a naming. Table 5.2 presents examples of the statistics that can be used with nominal scale data.

Ordinal scale. The ordinal scale is simply the nominal scale with one additional attribute: order. For instance, a productivity rating of 4 in year B would mean that a given program was more productive than in year A when it was rated at 2. The ratings identify different categories as in a nominal scale, but there is also an ordering. However, in the ordinal scale, the distance or interval between the items is not considered. The question of how much more productive in year B than in year A cannot be answered because of the rules used to assign the numbers. Other examples of ordinal scales are the Mohs scale for hardness of minerals and the quality scale for grade of leather. Harder minerals and higher-quality leather can be identified, but how much harder and how much better is not measured. With the ordinal scale, adding the same arbitrary constant to each number maintains the information content of the original numbers assigned (Table 5.1). The order is preserved, thus maintaining the ordinal scale. Origin is also an arbitrary parameter of the ordinal scale. Table 5.2 gives examples of statistics that can be used meaningfully with cardinal scale data.

Interval scale. The interval scale is simply the ordinal scale with one additional attribute: distance. The distance or interval between any two numbers on the scale can be identified and compared with the distance between any other two points on the scale. The origin in the interval scale is arbitrarily assigned. Examples of interval scales include time, calendars, and the temperature scales of Fahr-

Table 5.1 Scale Types

Scale Type	Example	Type of Relations Preserved	Admissible Transformations	Transformation Example*	Real-Number Characteristics Used
Nominal	Classed according to political party	Classification	Any 1 for 1	$m' = m$	
Ordinal	Grades of beef, wine	Classification plus transitivity	Monotonic increasing	$m' = m + a$	Order
Interval	Calendar time, temperature	Classification and transitivity plus additive intervals	Positive linear	$m' = a + bm$	Order, distance
Ratio	Population size, cash balance	Classification, transitivity, and additive intervals plus additive numbers (magnitudes)	Similarity	$m' = bm$	Order, distance, origin

*m = old measure
m' = transformed measure
a = an arbitrary constant
n = any other number
b = an arbitrary constant greater than zero

Source: Adapted from T. J. Mock and H. D. Grove, *Measurement, Accounting, and Organizational Information* (New York: John Wiley & Sons, 1979), p. 18.

Table 5.2 Examples of Permissible Statistics for Scale Types

Statistical Category	Nominal Scale	Ordinal Scale	Interval Scale	Ratio Scale
Measures of location	Mode	Median, mode	Arithmetic mean, median, mode	Arithmetic, geometric, and harmonic mean, median, mode
Measures of correlation	—	Rank-order (Spearman)	Rank-order, product-moment	Rank-order, product-moment
Significance tests	Chi square	Chi square, sign, run	Chi square, sign, run t, F	Chi square, sign, run t, F

Source: T. J. Mock and H. D. Grove, *Measurement, Accounting, and Organizational Information* (New York: John Wiley & Sons, 1979), p. 20.

enheit and Celsius. Any positive linear transformation of interval scale measurements will result in an equivalent set of interval scale measurement. Ratios of values on an interval scale are not meaningful because the origin is arbitrary—a matter of convention or convenience. For example, 80 degrees Celsius is not twice as hot as 40 degrees Celsius. Tables 5.1 and 5.2 present the major characteristics of the scale and examples of statistics that can be used meaningfully with interval scale data.

Ratio scale. The ratio scale is simply an interval scale with one additional attribute: unique origin. Given the unique origin or true zero point in a ratio scale, the only permissible transformation that will maintain the scale characteristics is multiplying the scale by a positive constant. The most obvious example of a ratio scale is numerosity—the actual count of some item—such as the amount of cash in the bank or the number of people in a room (see Table 5.1). All types of statistical measures are applicable to ratio scale data (see Table 5.2).

This discussion identifying the scales demonstrates that when numbers are assigned, not all of the inherent characteristics of the numbers may be represented in the resulting measurement. That is, there may or may not be a unique origin; the distance between observations may or may not be defined. That does not mean individuals will not use the data as if the parameters are defined. The numbers of an ordinal scale will be summed and divided by N to arrive at a mean value that of course is meaningless. The point is that awareness of the characteristics of the numbers used in a measurement scale is vital to meaningful use of the data. For example, it is senseless to use football-player jersey numbers as an indicator of relative value to the team. Within management control systems or elsewhere the information content of the measurements is a significant determinant of the appropriate use of the measurements.

Meaningfulness

One of the major concerns of the user of measurement information is that the statements made about the measurement information are meaningful. To be meaningful they must not exceed the inherent limitations of the data (Mock and Grove, 1979) and the reader must be able to understand them (Churchman, 1962). One example of exceeding the inherent limitations of data is using of the A-F classroom grading scale such that an A (4.0) represents twice the performance as a C (2.0). The grading scale is most definitely not a ratio scale. This grading scale will almost always meet the criteria for a nominal scale (the performance indicated by an A is different from the performance indicated by a B), will usually meet the criteria for an ordinal scale (where the performance indicated by an A is better than the performance indicated by a B), but will infrequently meet the criteria for an interval scale (in which the performance indicated by a B is midway between the performance indicated by an A and a C).

Churchman discusses meaningfulness in terms of finding a common language for measurement, that is, how is a scale going to be developed so that people can understand it? What words are to be used? Churchman's point is that the more precise the use of the words in describing the underlying concept, the fewer the people who will be able to understand the information the words convey. On the other hand, the more generally the words are understood, the more the precision of the information diminishes. For instance, if accountants use common terms to describe items on the balance sheet, more people would probably have some understanding of the balance sheet than if terms unique to accounting were used. However, because general terms (such as *cash*) are used, various definitions can be imputed to them. If accountants used the term *gzorts* for the same balance sheet item as *cash*, it would provide precise definition for those who understood what gzorts were, but it would be less generally useful to other people, who would be less likely to know the definition of gzorts. The reader would have to learn a special language in order to use the statements. Therein lies the language tradeoff.

Specification

Specification is the act of deciding on the scope of the application of the measurement (Churchman, 1962). What attributes are to be measured and under what circumstances can the measurements be made? Can changes in annual sales volume be used as a performance measure for the individuals who develop and place the corporate advertising? If the decision is no, some other measure will have to be identified. Whatever the measure is, a tradeoff must be made between the cost of the information and the potential return from such information. The goal is to have return exceed cost. The more generally applicable the measurement system (that is, useful for more applications), the more costly it will be. For instance, it would be useful to have a general measure of performance that could be used to evaluate the relative return on resources for all organizations. However, such a measure does not presently exist, and developing one would be a difficult and expensive task.

The availability of information will also influence what is measured. If information is needed (for example, performance information) by the tenth of the month but the accounting system will only produce it by the twentieth of the month, some surrogate data will be used (Ijiri, Jaedicke, and Knight, 1966). While the original information represents an attribute of the object of interest, the surrogate data are an approximation to the desired information and thus one step further removed from the object of interest.

What are surrogates and why are they used? A surrogate is simply a substitute. The measure of an attribute is a surrogate for the object of interest. Arrival at work on time, the number of letters typed, or the number of papers typed are surrogate measures of clerical performance because, as previously stressed, performance itself cannot be measured. As indicated in the model presented in Fig. 1.1, the attributes of performance measured could be viewed as the objects of interest. The surrogate in effect becomes the performance.

Standards

Given that most experiences take place in different times and different contexts, some means are needed to translate the experiences from one time and context to another. Will $50,000 per year provide for the same quality of life in New York City as it will in Seattle? Standards provide the basis for adjusting experiences in different contexts (Churchman, 1962). Developing standards balances two needs: the need for a minimum amount of adjustment and the need for precision. There is a tradeoff between adjustment and precision: the less adjustment necessary for a measure from one time and place to another, the less precise the measure is likely to be. The use of value added to the economy as a standard for market potential of a product requires a minimum amount of adjustment from one time and location to another. However, the degree of precision of this measure is not as high as other measures that require greater adjustment.

The standard can be viewed as a data reduction device that decreases and simplifies the amount of data required in a given situation. If standards did not exist, complete descriptions of the situation surrounding the object and attribute of interest would have to be given so that comparisons of the attributes could be made. If generally accepted accounting principles did not exist, much more information would be required to ensure the comparability of the financial statements of two organizations than is now the case. In order to compare management control systems, great amounts of information must be given. Why? One reason is that there is no clear standard that can be used to summarize the performance of one system at a given time and place such that it can be compared with another system at another time and place.

Reliability

To what degree do repeated measurements of the same attribute vary? This is a question of reliability. How much error is there in the measurement within the management control system of someone's performance? If a particular person is evaluated as being better than anybody else at a particular task, how reliable is that measure? The reliability of the data should influence the kind of decisions that are made with the data. Therefore, there must be some way to estimate reliability or accuracy. The challenge of accuracy is to develop measures that enable the user to evaluate the error contained in the measurement (Churchman, 1962, p. 139). The degree of accuracy will vary; the concern is not that error exists but that there be ways to identify, measure, and control the error (Mock and Grove, 1979).

Validity

Validity refers to the degree to which the relations among the numbers are the same as the actual relations among the quantities measured (Mock and Grove, 1979). In other words, validity concerns the relation between the measures and the attribute measured (Ijiri, Jaedicke, and Knight, 1966). If firm A shows twice as much depreciation on its financial statement than does firm B, and if firm A really has twice the economic depreciation of firm B, the assigned numbers are said to be valid measures of economic depreciation.

Types of measurement

The three types of measures—fundamental, derived, and fiat—are concerned with the sources of the measures. How have the measures come about? How did they get their meaning? Is it because of some fundamental measurement? Is it because two other fundamental measurements have been related? Is it because someone says so? *Fundamental* measurement is the direct measurement of extensions and attributes of objects (Stevens, 1946; Torgerson, 1967), such as a count of the number of widgets or a count of the cash. *Derived* measures are obtained by manipulating other measures. For instance, earnings per share is a derived measure. No one directly measures earnings per share; the values are determined by combining other measures. A large part of the results of an accounting system are derived measures. A third type of measurement is by *fiat:* the measure is simply defined to be what it is. For instance, learning ability is defined as the number of trials and errors required to accomplish a task. Other examples of fiat measures are depreciation and profit, two measures produced by the accounting system. Are the numbers on the bottom of an income statement the profits for the firm? Certainly. Why? Because the profits are calculated by using accounting techniques; therefore by definition that is the profit.

DEVELOPING MEASUREMENT SYSTEMS

Mock and Grove (1979) describe a five-step process to develop a system for measuring (Fig. 5.2). The first step is to identify the context and purpose for the measurement. This step may seem obvious; however, it is possible to develop a very sophisticated measurement system that has great specificity, validity, and reliability but is not very useful. Just because the measurement system is technically sound does not mean it is useful. Very sophisticated ratio-scale measurements may not be able to serve a need for promptness as well as nominal-scale measurements could. For example, in production runs, whether a part falls within specifications or not must be determined rapidly. If the part is outside of specifications, it must be rejected. An elaborate process that tells how far outside of specifications rejected parts fall could be useful but is probably not worth the expense of slowing down the rejection process.

Step two is to identify the relevant attributes to be measured. Let us say that an organization is interested in controlling personnel costs. What attributes of personnel should be measured—the number of personnel working for the organization on a particular

Figure 5.2 Framework for Measurement System Development

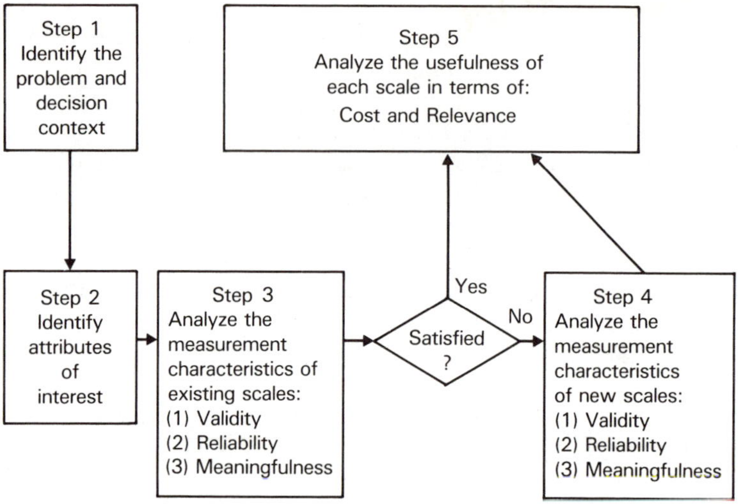

```
┌─────────────────┐              ┌──────────────────────────────┐
│ Step 1          │              │ Step 5                       │
│ Identify the    │              │ Analyze the usefulness of    │
│ problem and     │              │ each scale in terms of:      │
│ decision        │              │ Cost and Relevance           │
│ context         │              │                              │
└─────────────────┘              └──────────────────────────────┘
                                        ▲               ▲
                                        │ Yes           │
┌─────────┐  ┌──────────────────┐   ┌───────┐   ┌──────────────────┐
│ Step 2  │  │ Step 3           │   │       │No │ Step 4           │
│ Identify│  │ Analyze the      │   │Satis- │──▶│ Analyze the      │
│attributes│─▶│ measurement      │──▶│ fied  │   │ measurement      │
│ of      │  │ characteristics  │   │  ?    │   │ characteristics  │
│ interest│  │ of existing      │   │       │   │ of new scales:   │
│         │  │ scales:          │   └───────┘   │ (1) Validity     │
│         │  │ (1) Validity     │               │ (2) Reliability  │
│         │  │ (2) Reliability  │               │ (3) Meaningfulness│
│         │  │ (3) Meaningfulness│              │                  │
└─────────┘  └──────────────────┘               └──────────────────┘
```

Source: Adapted from T. J. Mock and H. D. Grove, *Measurement, Accounting, and Organizational Information* (New York: John Wiley & Sons, 1979), p. 36.

day? What would happen if the count were taken on the one day of the year when a number of the employees were laid off? Measuring this one attribute obviously does not provide all the information desired, but it appears to be an important one, so counting people probably makes sense. What else needs to be measured? Maybe counting the total number of hours worked by employees within the operation for the year will capture an important attribute. However, suppose most of the work was accomplished on contract. Perhaps the gross number of service contracts needs to be measured. To control personnel costs, then, one probably must consider people, hours, and dollars allocated to service contracts. Identifying the relevant attributes is one of the most difficult tasks in the measurement process.

Evaluating the factual aspects of existing measures is the third step in Mock and Grove's framework. The factual aspects are concerned with reliability, meaningfulness, and validity. If the existing measures meet these criteria, then the development process is complete. If not, the fourth step is to develop new scales that will work—to construct and analyze a new measurement system from the factual point of view.

The final step is to evaluate the cost and relevance of the measurement system to be used. In all cases the value of the measurement information should be greater than the cost of acquisition. Alternative measurements will probably be available in most situations. Knowing the planned use of the measurement information provides the criteria that can be used to define the most relevant measurement system for the problem at hand. The cost of such a system can then be determined and compared with potential relevance.

These five steps are useful tools to guide the development of measurement systems that provide the information for use in planning, control, and evaluation.

FUNCTIONAL FIXATION

What are some of the implications of measurement systems and changes in measurement systems for managerial behavior? Ijiri, Jaedicke, and Knight (1966) address one issue: functional fixation, which occurs when an individual identifies some measure of an attribute as having a specific meaning. If the meaning changes, the person does not recognize what the change is or even that the change has occurred and as a result will make faulty decisions.

Let us say that a supervisor, Jan, wishes to base the evaluation of a department head, Terry, on the amount of work accomplished by the department. Part (a) of Fig. 5.3 depicts this relationship. Jan recognizes that the amount of work accomplished has many attributes or dimensions but defines the amount of work only as the dollar value of job orders completed. This measure then becomes a surrogate for the amount of work accomplished by the department. Part (b) of Fig. 5.3 depicts this relationship. However, the dollar value of the job orders completed is based on cost inputs from the accounting system. Part (c) of Fig. 5.3 depicts this relationship. Let us say that, when Jan chose the dollar value of job orders completed as the surrogate for the amount of work accomplished, plant depreciation was not included as a cost input but at a later date it

Figure 5.3 Example of Functional Fixation

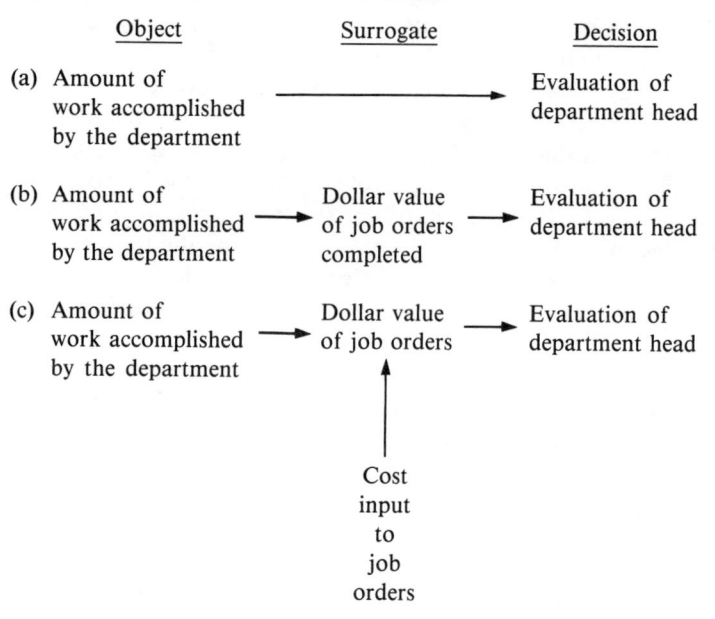

	Object	Surrogate	Decision
(a)	Amount of work accomplished by the department	→	Evaluation of department head
(b)	Amount of work accomplished by the department	→ Dollar value of job orders completed →	Evaluation of department head
(c)	Amount of work accomplished by the department	→ Dollar value of job orders ↑ Cost input to job orders →	Evaluation of department head

was. If Jan is unable or does not adjust the evaluation decision to the change in the surrogate measure, functional fixation has occurred. An additional dimension to the analysis is that even if Terry can adjust to the change in the surrogate, Jan's functional fixation may lead to undesirable consequences. If Terry's goal is to maintain a consistent level of output as evaluated by Jan (that is, work accomplished by the department as measured by the dollar value of job orders completed), less work will have to be accomplished assuming constant resource inputs.

SUMMARY

The function of measurement is to develop a method of generating a class of information that will be useful for a wide variety of problems and situations. To do so, one must first establish a series of definitions: What is wide? What is information? Information to whom? What is the appropriate scale of measurement? The generation of the information will entail a number of decisions—indeed, measurement is a decision process (Churchman, 1962).

SUGGESTED READINGS

American Accounting Association. Report of Committee on Internal Measurement and Reporting. *The Accounting Review, Supplement,* 1973, *48,* 208-223.

Churchman, C. West. Why Measure? In C. West Churchman and Philburn Ratoosh (Eds.). *Measurement Definitions and Theories.* New York: John Wiley & Sons, 1962, pp. 83-94.

Ijiri, Yuji. *Studies in Accounting Research*, No. 10: *Theory of Accounting Measurement.* Sarasota, Fla.: American Accounting Association, 1975.

Mock, Theodore J. and Hugh D. Grove. *Measurement Accounting and Information.* New York: John Wiley & Sons, 1979.

Stevens, S. S. On the theory of scales of measurement. *Science,* June 1946, *103*(2685), 677-680.

Chapter Six

THEORY

EXPLAINING REALITY
A SECOND EXPLANATION
Syntactics
Semantics
Pragmatics
Empirical and Nonempirical Sciences
THE RELATIONSHIP
THE CASE FOR INTUITION
THEORY FORMULATION
THE VERIFICATION PROCESS
DECISION MAKING
Theory Verification and Measurement
SUMMARY
SUGGESTED READINGS

Thus far this text has taken the reader from a general discussion of management control systems through the more specific topics of planning, control, evaluation, and measurement. The discussion of each topic was intended to contribute to an understanding of the problems associated with the design, implementation, and operation of management control systems. The model presented in Chapter One depicts an organization influenced by specific situational contingencies that, along with the organization's goals and objectives, indicate the appropriate characteristics for the management control system. Specific outcomes of that system are then identified, and attributes of those outcomes are measured. These measures become the focus of attention within the organization, influencing both the behavior of the individuals operating within the system—whose performance the measures were designed to evaluate—and the system itself.

The model depicted in Fig. 1.1 is similar to other management control models and has empirical support. Caveats relating to each of the elements and relationships depicted in the model were given in the previous chapters. However, positive guidance relating to the elements and relationships is more difficult to identify. Why? One reason is that the model of management control presented in Fig. 1.1 is based on theories that are not fully developed. If they were completely developed, the design, implementation, and operation of management control systems would be a precise science, producing predictable results. However, such is not the case.

This chapter describes what theories in general are and how they are developed. Understanding this contributes to a better understanding of the design, implementation, and operation of management control systems. This chapter begins with a discussion of what a theory is and then an examination of theory development and verification, emphasizing the importance of intuition in science. Finally, the relationship between decision making and developing a theory of planning, control, and evaluation is presented.

EXPLAINING REALITY

A theory can be defined as "a systematically related set of statements, including some lawlike generalizations, that is empirically testable" (Rudner, 1966, p. 10). There are few terms in the scientific lexicon whose use, both by scientists and nonscientists, is in such an anarchic state as the term *theory*. The use of the term *theory* in this text is consistent with Rudner (1966). However, his definition of a theory leaves nonempirical areas of study devoid of theories. These areas, by contrast, possess axiomatic systems. An axiomatic system is a set of interrelated analytic concepts or constructs that are internally self-consistent and do not necessarily have empirical validity (Rudner, 1966). Accounting is an example. Following the rules of accounting will generate answers. However, the answers do not necessarily have anything to do with reality or observations but are simply based on a set of internally consistent concepts or constructs.

Empirical relationships distinguish an axiomatic system from a theory. Said another way, a theory is an axiomatic system with empirical validity. Measurement, the subject of the previous chapter, is the means by which the theory is verified. For an axiomatic system, measurement is not necessary. The relationships among the constructs are not measured. The logic either is or is not valid. Figure 5.1 is useful for demonstrating the distinction between a theory and an axiomatic system. If it is possible in Fig. 5.1 to start at A and work to F in a logically consistent way, the axiomatic system holds. Mathematics is an example of an axiomatic system because it does not necessarily have anything to do with external reality (even though it can be used in and applied to the physical world).

The constructs of mathematics are internally consistent, self-contained, and not dependent on empirical observations. Plane geometry can be used as an axiomatic system. However, if one applies plane geometry to external reality or the realm of observation (Fig. 5.1), plane geometry now becomes a theory, to the extent that the axiomatic system is tied by means of observations to reality.

The observations are related to the constructs by means of operational definitions or rules of correspondence, which help to verify the empirical truth of the purely axiomatic constructs. The empirical verification of the axiomatic system provides a means of relating two different empirical observations. For instance, a physicist can take measurements of the heat and volume of some gas, heat the gas to some specific temperature, and predict what the new volume and pressure of the gas will be. The physicist is empirically verifying a theory, at least in a limited sense. However, as discussed previously, not all theories allow such precise prediction: those that do are said to be well explicated; those that do not are not well explicated.

In general, well-explicated theories (Fig. 5.1) are found in the physical sciences, while theories in the social sciences (Fig. 6.1) tend not to be as well explicated. Torgerson (1967), states theories in the social sciences do not consist of all the neat, solid connections from construct to construct; the relationships are not totally explicated. The dotted lines indicate that relationships between the constructs exist but that the exact relationships between the constructs are not fully understood. This means that observing I does not necessarily allow one to predict E. However, most well-explicated theories start out tenuously. Early physical scientists such as Galileo, Copernicus, and Archimedes helped to identify, in their respective disciplines, relationships that connect the constructs. The same is now happening in the social sciences. For instance, the work of Skinner (1978) is just such an effort. However, using the measurement of a specific behavior to predict some other behavior may or may not be possible. Doing so raises the problems of incomplete explication of the relationships among the constructs and of the inadequate identification of rules of correspondence, as discussed in Chapter Five.

Figure 6.1 Illustration of a Typical Structure in the Social and Behavioral Sciences

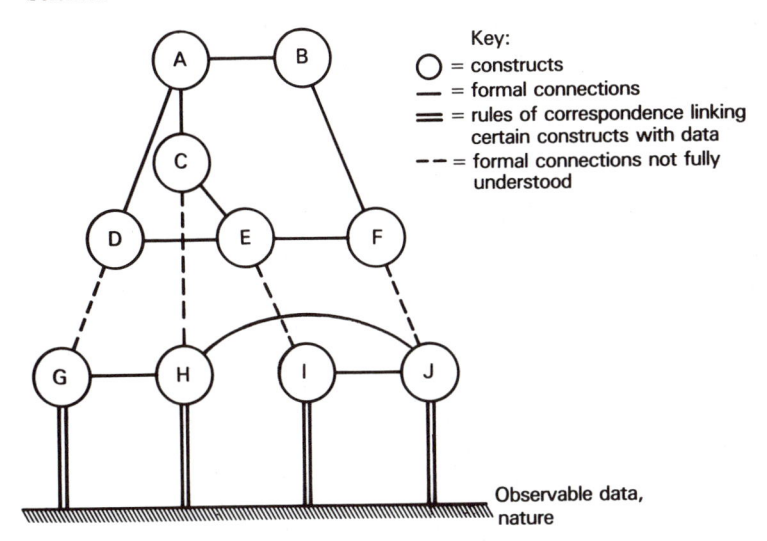

Key:
○ = constructs
— = formal connections
═ = rules of correspondence linking certain constructs with data
-- = formal connections not fully understood

Observable data, nature

Source: Adapted from W. S. Torgerson, *Theory and Methods of Scaling* (New York: John Wiley & Sons, 1967), p. 5.

A SECOND EXPLANATION

A theory can also be defined as a set of sentences governed by the three major areas of language study: syntactics, semantics, and pragmatics (Sterling, 1970). This definition helps to highlight further the components of a theory.

Syntactics

Syntactics is the study of the relationships between signs—sounds or visual symbols produced by a person to communicate with and influence someone else (Carnap, 1955)—and the rules governing the use of signs. Axiomatic systems are totally in the realm of syntactics. The sign relationship rules say nothing about observed reality; math and logic emphasize purely logical relationships and do not necessarily have anything to do with meaning. For example, if all *gflxes* have *zang* and *whiblet m* has no *zang*, then *whiblet m* is not a *gflx*. There is no need to know the meanings of *gflx, zang,* or *whiblet m*. By the syntactic rules of logic, *whiblet m* has been determined to be something other than a *gflx* (Sterling, 1970).

Semantics

Semantics is the study of the relationship between signs and objects or events. Semantic rules give empirical meaning to the signs through definition. Rules of correspondence are semantic rules. Using the semantic rules, which link signs to events or objects, and the syntactic rules, which link signs to signs, one can make statements with empirical content. These statements, unlike purely syntactic propositions, have the potential for empirical verification. For example, the statement, "All red streetcars go to Garden Park," intends to say something about a thing in the real world. *Red streetcars* is a sign for something in the world, and the proposition states something definitive about them (Sterling, 1970).

Pragmatics

Pragmatics is the study of the relationship between the signs and their users. Different signs may evoke different responses from the same user even though the signs are meant to refer to the same object or construct. For example, Lou needing something to tighten a screw in a kitchen chair, goes to the kitchen tool drawer to find a screwdriver. In the drawer Lou finds a hammer, a pair of pliers, a collection of assorted change, and some old keys. Frustrated, Lou walks down to the hardware store to purchase a screwdriver. However, keys or coins could also be used to tighten a screw in a kitchen chair. In this situation, a screwdriver, coins, and keys are all signs with the same referent.

Different users of the same sign may interpret that same sign differently (Sterling, 1970). The definition of *money* ("M1") used by the Federal Reserve Bank may be known by some individuals, but for many *money* takes on diverse meanings.

Empirical and nonempirical sciences

Using the distinctions of syntactics, semantics, and pragmatics, sciences may be classified as empirical or nonempirical (Sterling, 1970). Empirical sciences are those in which the truth value of propositions or statements depends on occurrences in the real world and are used for the prediction and explanation of occurrences in the real world. According to Rudner's definition, these sciences have theories. Examples of empirical sciences are chemistry, archaeology, and sociology. Nonempirical sciences, on the other hand, are composed entirely of analytic propositions, or axioms, and do not depend on empirical findings for their truth value. Logic and mathematics are examples of nonempirical sciences.

Theories in the empirical sciences have parts that can be identified as syntactic, semantic, and pragmatic. The syntactic part of an empirical theory is represented by an axiomatic system—a set of signs that are internally consistent and do not depend on empirical verification for their truth value. Semantic rules link the signs of the axiomatic system to observable objects or events. This linking allows for empirical verification of the theory. However, not all of the statements or propositions of the theory will be empirically verifiable.

Nonempirical sciences have only axiomatic systems constructed of analytic statements or propositions that are in the syntactic domain. There are no semantic rules in axiomatic systems.

Sterling (1970) uses geometry as a means to demonstrate the difference between an empirical and a nonempirical science. Geometry can be studied as a nonempirical science, consisting only of a set of axioms, which have no referents in the real world. To give geometry empirical meaning, semantic rules are used to operationalize primitive (undefined) terms such as *point* and *straight line*. A point is defined as the crossing of two lines on the tip of a surveyor's stake. A straight line is operationalized as a taut string on the path of a ray of light. Now that the formal system of geometry has been given referents in the real world it becomes an empirical theory, it can be used to explain and predict events, for example, that the exterior angle of a triangle is greater than either nonadjacent interior angle. The theory specifies the information necessary to prove the theorem, and the results can be verified through a separate empirical operation.

Figure 6.2 presents Sterling's depiction of a theory. The theory is composed of inputs and outputs that are connected by syntactic manipulation. The inputs, syntactic manipulation, and outputs exist at the axiomatic level. They are given empirical meaning via semantic connections, which relate the axiomatic part of the theory to observable events and objects on the observation plane. The inputs to the model can be expressed as some type of measurement (for example, dollars, pounds, or height). These inputs can then be manipulated with the syntactic rules, which in turn will produce output, which can be related back to the observation realm.

A slightly more complex model of an empirical science (Fig. 6.3) is adapted from the Committee on Accounting Theory Construction and Verification of the American Accounting Association. The model expands on the simpler model presented by Sterling by presenting the syntactic manipulations as a series of separate entities. The semantic rules translate observations into inputs that are usable within the formal model. The inputs to this manipulative system generate outputs used in some type of prediction model. In turn, the outputs of the prediction model are used as inputs to a decision model. The decision then results in some action

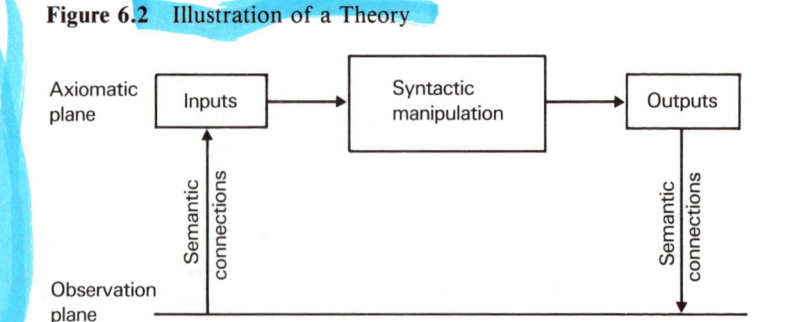

Figure 6.2 Illustration of a Theory

Source: Adapted from R. R. Sterling, On theory construction and verification, *Accounting Review,* July 1970, *45*(3), p. 448.

Figure 6.3 Illustration of the Relationship of Inputs to Prediction and Decision Processes

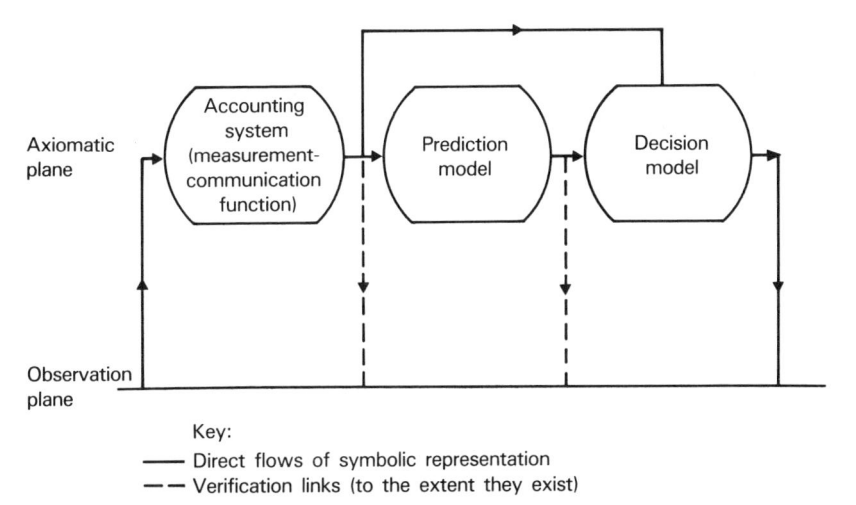

```
                  ┌──────────────┐      ┌──────────┐      ┌──────────┐
                  │ Accounting   │      │          │      │          │
 Axiomatic        │ system       │      │Prediction│      │ Decision │
 plane            │(measurement- │─────▶│  model   │─────▶│  model   │────▶
                  │communication │      │          │      │          │
                  │  function)   │      │          │      │          │
                  └──────┬───────┘      └────┬─────┘      └────┬─────┘
                         ▲  │                │                 │
                         │  ▼                ▼                 ▼
 Observation ────────────┴──────────────────────────────────────────
 plane
```

Key:
──── Direct flows of symbolic representation
── ── Verification links (to the extent they exist)

Source: Adapted from American Accounting Association, Report of the Committee on Accounting Theory Construction and Verification, *Accounting Review, Supplement,* 1971, *46,* p. 60.

that is observable. As the diagram indicates, the measurement information may not be an input to a prediction model but may still directly affect the decision.

THE RELATIONSHIP

How does this discussion relate to planning, control, or evaluation? Planning, control, and evaluation are concerned with affecting behavior and operations within the decision process. Measurements are taken and processed to become inputs to a predictive model, which then produces inputs to a decision model. The decision model in turn results in some action. The planning, control, and evaluation system is used to make specific predictions of what will happen in the future. Planning, control, and evaluation is premised on measurements that influence predictions in decision models, thereby resulting in desired behavior. If one is to predict using a planning, control, and evaluation system, it is necessary not only to have some kind of measurement system but also to understand the relevant prediction and decision models. Therefore, if organizational planning, control, and evaluation are to be effective, the relevant psychological and social constructs must be understood. Because the relationships among these constructs are not well understood, the ability of planning, control, and evaluation cycles to operate effectively and efficiently is questionable. It is important to recognize that an incomplete understanding of the fundamental relationships underlies the processes necessary for management control systems. Recognizing this should help to develop a richer appreciation for the basic imprecision inherent in any management control system on the part of those individuals who interact with management control systems. Quite simply, if one understands the strengths and weaknesses of a system's foundation, one is better able to facilitate or frustrate the system.

THE CASE FOR INTUITION

In a theory that is not well explicated, intuition serves a purpose. Intuition can incorporate variables whose connections are represented by the dotted lines depicted in Torgerson's model (Fig. 6.1).

Although techniques of research and theorization excel in rigorous analysis, they are weak in their sensitivity to the "subtleties of human existence that are predominantly important in human behavior" (Gerboth, 1973, p. 476). This is especially true in the decision process. He points out that effort is too often expended on inputs and outputs that can be measured rather than on those that are less quantifiable but far more important in the decision process. While these latter measures cannot be explicitly assessed, "and, consequently, cannot be effectively considered in systematic analysis," they are "generally more useful in explaining and predicting human behavior than is knowledge that can be made explicit" (Gerboth, 1973, p. 476).

Gerboth makes a strong case for intuition. The real goal of research and theorization is to describe the decision process and not just the planning, control, and evaluation processes. Intuition can aid in research because it is able to process knowledge not amenable to analysis. Gerboth's view is that the "human brain is as yet unequaled in its ability to draw on inarticulate knowledge of fashions, mores, traditions, climates of opinion, and other obscure forces at work in human affairs" (1973, p. 476). In other words, intuition is able to identify relationships between constructs that have not or cannot be identified using current analytic techniques. Selecting appropriate management control system components and performance measures can to a degree be aided by theory, but where theory weakens, intuition becomes a useful (and possibly stronger) guide.

Gerboth points out that intuition on the one hand and theorization and research on the other are complementary approaches to decision theory. Accounting provides information "that enhances a decision-maker's capacity for judgment, not to make the judgment for him" (Gerboth, p. 447). Intuition fills the gaps left by analysis and, by so doing, can become the means by which a theory begins to develop. The tentative theory can represent intuitions that are formulated and then empirically tested.

THEORY FORMULATION

As the previous discussion indicates, theories do not initially appear in their full glory as Venus did. It takes many hours of effort to turn bare ideas into tested theory. Developing the theory depends on devising tentative or hypothetical statements of important relationships between constructs. It is necessary to consider only the important relationships because it is impractical to investigate all possible relationships. This need implies an a priori effort in order to formulate hypotheses, which will be based on observation plus intuition. Essential for the orderly development of a theory is a well-defined hypothesis, the means by which alternative explanations of relationships can be eliminated. The development of management control systems implicitly assumes that some explanations of reality will hold and others will not. These explanations in effect are hypotheses that, when tested, help to explicate the theory underlying management control.

THE VERIFICATION PROCESS

The processes of theory development and theory verification are intertwined steps in an iterative process. Building a theory requires that new constructs added to it have an experimentally testable reference so that they may be verified (Rudner, 1966).

In general, most social sciences appear to possess theoretical propositions about observable phenomena that are not subject to the control of the investigator (Williams and Griffin, 1969). Theory verification in the social sciences, as well as the physical sciences, requires that deduced results correspond to observable phenomena.

The primary complication in social science theory is human behavior, which makes replication of a situation difficult if not impossible. Therefore, theory verification may be less conclusive in the social sciences than in the physical sciences. However, the degree of verification may be sufficient to corroborate the theory (Williams and Griffin, 1969).

Theory development is aimed at identifying truth and making the unexpected expected and thus is oriented towards achieving some predictive capability. The predictive capability of theory is examined by the process of verification. In any absolute sense, verification is impossible, since theories cannot address themselves to the total sum of all relationships. The theories abstract the relevant factors and attempt to explain outputs based on inputs. The best abstraction is the one that best captures the relevant aspects of reality (American Accounting Association, 1971).

The Committee on Internal Measurement and Reporting of the American Accounting Association summarizes the four ways of verifying or fixing belief about the truth value of a hypothesis as developed by Cohen and Nagel (1934):

Method of tenacity—believing something is true because one has always known it to be true.

Method of authority—accepting something as true because some authority says it is true.

Method of intuition—accepting something as true because it is self-evident or agrees with intuitive reason.

Method of science—accepting something as true because it has been demonstrated by methods which are objectively determined—withstanding self-correcting analysis and examination (American Accounting Association, 1973, p. 215).

For the purposes of theory verification, the first three methods are unreliable. However, in the fourth method it is not at all apparent that something can be objectively determined. Notwithstanding this reservation, the method of science has the highest potential for conclusiveness in the creation of knowledge. If used at all, the method of science must be applied to the entire process, from idea formulation through analysis of the data. The Committee on Internal Measurement (1973) divides this process into four stages:

1. *The idea.* An idea originates from a wide spectrum of human experiences. The concern is not so much with the origin of the idea, but rather with additional effort required to validate it.
2. *Theory building.* In this step, theories are created, propositions are put forth, and models are established. From these, hypotheses are nominated for testing.
3. *Data gathering.* The testing of theories and hypotheses requires some means of gathering the data predetermined to be pertinent to validation. Data requirements or collection methods must be decided in view of the uses to which they will be put.
4. *Data analysis.* Data analysis entails using appropriate analytical or statistical techniques that will both capitalize on the information inherent in the data available and provide the type of evidence to reject or not reject a hypothesis.

Though the method of science should be applied to each of the steps, intuition can facilitate each step. As Lightman has so aptly stated, "Although it is almost pure left-hemisphere stuff, first-rate scientific work must often include an intuitive factor" (1982, p. 28).

DECISION MAKING

In order to capture the relevant aspects of reality as depicted in Fig. 6.3, the decision-making process must be included either implicitly or explicitly in any theory that purports to deal with planning, control, and evaluation.

The Committee on Internal Measurement and Reporting of the American Accounting Association summarize Forrester's (1962) division of management decisions into four groups:

1. Automatic-decisions made by machine, such as payroll checks (programmed decision)
2. Decisions guided by incomplete policy—most middle management decisions made according to well understood guiding policy
3. Based on experience, intuition, judgment—top management decisions not covered by policy although there is some presumption as to what constitutes proper action
4. Baffling, unexplored, not attempted—no basis for action (American Accounting Association, 1973, p. 212).

The probability of accurately describing the use of information by the decision maker decreases progressively from group 1 to group 4. As the decisions become more complex and human judgment more prominent in the decision process, it becomes harder to define and understand the parameters of the process. Notice that in each succeeding type of decision there is decreasing evidence of an identifiable structure for the decision process. The decision makers become more loosely coupled with whatever comes before and after them. For each situation there is also more than one way to achieve the desired objective as suggested by the concept of equifinality. The managers are in an open-systems context, each using selected resource inputs in various ways to achieve the same goal.

At the lower end of the four categories (group 1), where things are very precisely defined, the managers have little flexibility to select inputs or process. Information needs and uses are more obvious here than at the higher levels. Compatibility between the goals of the decision maker and those of the organization becomes increasingly important as one moves from group 1 to group 4. If the managers have the same goals as the organization or are rewarded when the organization achieves its goals, the decision makers will be motivated to seek and process information such as to benefit both themselves and the organization.

This discussion implicitly assumes that goal compatibility is a vehicle to obviate problems. Assuming the goal-compatibility hypothesis to be true, won't there be a measurement problem? For instance, profit sharing helps manipulate or motivate managers to exhibit behaviors that are good for the organization. However, there is a larger question: is profit, as measured by the accounting system, the goal of the organization? Or is the goal long-run wealth maximization? If it is the latter, aren't the managers all heading in the wrong direction by chasing profit? Thus the degree to which the managers will respond to the specific reward offered becomes increasingly important in the decision process as the scope goes from the programmed to the baffling and unexplored. This requires more input of behavior variables into the theory.

Theory verification and measurement

The Committee on Accounting Theory Construction and Verification of the American Accounting Association (1971) points out problems in measurement related to theory verification:

1. The decision process—and thus what information should be measured—may not be ascertainable.
2. Numerous alternative measures may exist without the measurer knowing which set provides the best measurement.
3. Prediction variables are often measured in more than one way.
4. Bias in favor of readily available measures may exist.

The four problems link the discussion in Chapter Five to the discussion of theory development and verification in this chapter. Theory development and verification cannot be conducted unless the appropriate measures exist.

SUMMARY

This chapter guided the reader through theory construction and verification. Certainly a case can be made that any theory purporting to explain planning, control, or evaluation must implicitly or explicitly identify the interactions of these with the decision process, since planning, control, and evaluation all produce inputs to the decision process.

The topics of theory construction and verification go hand in hand. Axiomatic systems purporting to explain empirical phenomena are useless without verification, and a purely syntactic or logic-oriented verification simply will not suffice for models of planning, control, or evaluation.

SUGGESTED READINGS

American Accounting Association. Report of Committee on Accounting Theory Construction and Verification. *The Accounting Review, Supplement,* 1971, *46,* 50-79.

Cohen, Morris R. and Ernest Nagel. *An Introduction to Logic and Scientific Method.* London: Routledge & Kegan Paul, 1934.

Dewey, John. *How We Think.* Boston: D. C. Heath, 1910.

Kuhn, Thomas S. *The Structure of Scientific Revolutions* (2nd Edition). In Otto Neurath (Ed.). *International Encyclopedia of Unified Science,* Vol. 2, No. 2. Chicago: University of Chicago Press, 1970.

Margenau, Henry. *The Nature of Physical Reality.* New York: McGraw-Hill Book Company, 1950.

Popper, Karl R. *Objective Knowledge.* Oxford: Oxford University Press, 1972.

Rudner, Richard S. *Philosophy of Social Science.* Englewood Cliffs, N.J.: Prentice-Hall, 1966.

Schrader, William J. and Robert E. Malcom. A note on accounting theory construction and verification. *Abacus,* June 1973, *9,* 93-98.

Skinner, B. F. *Reflections on Behaviorism and Society.* Englewood Cliffs, N.J.: Prentice-Hall, 1978.

Sterling, Robert R. On theory construction and verification. *The Accounting Review,* July 1970, *45*(3), 444-457.

Chapter Seven

THE DESIGN OF MANAGEMENT CONTROL SYSTEMS

DESIGN CONSIDERATIONS
Goals and Objectives
Attributes Measured
Manipulation
Timing
Bottom Up and Top Down
Outside Support
The Designers
Line versus Staff Needs
External Reporting Needs
Resistance
THE MANAGEMENT CONTROL SYSTEM AND THE OPERATING ENVIRONMENT
SUMMARY
SELECTED READINGS

The purpose of this chapter is to present an overview of management control systems design. Design factors that must be considered are discussed, and the distinction between the science and art of systems design is highlighted.

One way to view an organization is as a system with goals and objectives that processes inputs and generates outputs. A key component of that process is the management control system. As depicted in Fig. 1.1, management control is a means of relating an organization's goals to its outputs and the outputs to the planning system. Management control is different from planning, measurement, and evaluation, and it involves more than simply identifying the operational controls. As demonstrated in Chapter One, a control system may be operating as designed, but management control will not necessarily be achieved. Management control is "a pragmatic concern for results, obtained through people" (Hofstede, 1981, p. 193). More formally, it is "the process by which managers assure that resources are obtained and used effectively and efficiently in the accomplishment of the organization's objectives" (Anthony, 1965, p. 17). Management control supports and relies on the functions of planning, control, evaluation, and measurement. However, doing each of these functions appropriately does not assure that the management control system will be functional, because there is no well-explicated theory to guide its development and operation.

DESIGN CONSIDERATIONS

Management control systems are designed and do function. What are some of the requisite considerations for their design? The organization's technology, environment, employees, and size are all factors that can influence the effectiveness of the management control system (Lawler and Rhode, 1976). However, even an apparently well-designed system can be used ineffectively or have unanticipated results.

Ansari (1977) describes two approaches to the analysis of management control system design: the structural and the behavioral. The structural view is essentially mechanistic, focusing on information networks and communicating the information. This approach has been adopted by researchers in cybernetics, accounting, and management information systems. Implicit in the structural approach is the assumption that, if the system is appropriately designed, people will respond in the appropriate or prescribed fashion. Behavior that is not appropriate is viewed as essentially random or idiosyncratic. The behavioral approach stresses concern for motivating the individual. The management control system is viewed as one of many systems that interact with individuals, who make choices based on their particular goals and needs. Ansari argues that both approaches to design must be used. Do these approaches explain how to design a system? No. They do, however, call attention to both the structure of the management control system and the resulting behavior. They should also help the designer identify personal bias that may enter into the design of the system. Therefore, the discussion in this chapter will focus on both the structure and the behavioral impact of the system.

The following sections discuss key areas of concern—as identified in the literature on the subject—in the design of management control systems.

Goals and objectives

Are goals and objectives important? Evidence indicates they should be clear, reasonably specific, so that employees have a clear idea of what is expected of them, and at an appropriate level of difficulty

(Kenis, 1979; Kerr and Slocum, 1981). The appropriate level of difficulty for goals and objectives is not easily identifiable. The goals and objectives should be neither too loose nor too tight: they should be appropriate. This statement is simple, but accomplishing it is another matter. Easily attainable goals and objectives fail to present a challenge to the employee and therefore have little motivational effect. On the other hand, very tight and unattainable goals and objectives lead to feelings of failure, frustration, lower aspiration levels, and, finally, rejection of the goals and objectives by the participant. *Appropriate* could be defined as goals and objectives that are tight but attainable (Hofstede, 1967).

From a practical standpoint the development of appropriate goals and objectives requires the participation of the evaluated person and of the evaluator. The argument for cooperative setting of goals and objectives is nothing new (Drucker, 1954; Odiorne, 1965). However, cooperation must be used carefully. When goals and objectives are being developed for purposes of distributing extrinsic rewards such as pay, the people being evaluated may be motivated to give invalid data about how well they can perform. Obviously, low-level goals and objectives create a greater chance for receiving rewards than do high-level goals and objectives. Research on topics such as piece-rate incentive systems indicates that the reporting of false information indeed occurs. Subsequent standards are then set too low to be intrinsically motivating (Lawler and Rhode, 1976). Setting goals and objectives for extrinsic reward, must therefore be handled with great care to insure that the goals and objectives or standards are of sufficient difficulty.

Developing the goals or objectives jointly implies a level of participation by the person being evaluated. Research supports the argument that participation is related to satisfaction of the person being evaluated or the person participating (Milani, 1975; Swieringa and Moncur, 1975). Though the relationship between participation and job performance is relatively weak (Milani, 1975; Kenis, 1979), the research indicates that participation, to the extent that it leads to goal clarity and the appropriate level of goal difficulty, will be reflected in performance (Kenis, 1979).

One can argue that goals and objectives are the results rather than the causes of actions. First there is action, and then goals, objectives, and related plans become the justifications for those actions (Weick, 1969). Goals and objectives are initially vague and become more specific only after one can review actions and results. The management control system provides the information that in effect legitimizes what the organization is doing (Cooper, Hayes, and Wolf, 1981). The proposed goals are expected to help direct the organization, but to the extent that experience does not fit with what is expected, expectations will be revised. These revisions can result in a reinterpretation of the goals and objectives or a totally different set of goals and objectives, and can necessitate an adjustment to the measures used within the management control system.

Attributes measured

The specific outputs that result from goals and objectives in turn are defined in terms of performance measures. Ideally the goals and objectives are directly measurable. However, it is highly unlikely that they, or even the specific outcomes, can be specified in such a manner. The measures of performance are measures of attributes. Unless performance is defined as an attribute, the measure of performance will be incomplete because the essence of performance is not measured. Given that the performance measures are tied to the organizational reward system, they will affect worker motivation. Lawler and Rhode (1976) identify three aspects of performance measures that affect motivation: completeness, objectivity, and influence. *Completeness* is concerned with the degree to which the attributes measured capture the essence of performance. Incomplete measures can miss key attributes of performance. The lack of measurement, evaluation, and subsequent rewards can lead workers to ignore the unmeasured attributes of performance. However, complete measures may be resisted because they may reduce autonomy or make individuals "look bad." *Objectivity* involves the extent to which the measure is impartial and cannot be manipulated. The lack of objectivity can result in manipulating the system in order to provide positive information for evaluation. On the other hand, objective measures may lead to efforts at "looking good" in terms of the attributes measured while ignoring attributes not measured. *Influence* is concerned with the degree to which the worker can effect the level of the measure. Measures that cannot be influenced can lead to resistance to or sabotage of the system and to the generation of invalid data. Ability to influence measures can lead workers to concentrate only on affecting those measures.

One of the criteria for choosing the performance measures must be the minimization of the difficulties just discussed. If a balanced set of measures is developed that overcomes these problems, won't creativity then be stifled, while historically successful behavior is imitated? A balanced and well-documented management control system can provide the information necessary to support consistent, goal-directed behavior that imitates past success. Such a system helps provide for the stability necessary in any organization, but the tradeoff is a possible stifling of creativity (Cooper, Hayes, and Wolf, 1981). If individuals do not overly respect the historical data, innovation can occur. As one of my students has quipped, the U.S. Navy prides itself on 200 years of tradition unmarked by progress—a condition that may have a lot to do with a high regard for historical data. The argument raises an interesting dilemma. History is the only traditional means to predict the future. If it is disregarded, a random walk results, but if it becomes the guide, freedom can be lost.

March (1976) argues that managers need to be able to do things that the organization as a whole does not support. This "heretical" behavior is a way for organizations to find new ways of doing things. However, if the measures of performance are well specified and rules are adhered to, this type of creative behavior will be stifled. A good set of performance measures would achieve a balance of completeness, objectivity, and ability to influence, yet be sufficiently ambiguous to allow some freedom to practice the "technology of foolishness," to use March's words.

Manipulation

Why the concern for reaction to the system? A primary reason for the existence of a management control system is to manipulate the behavior of people (Tosi, 1975). Management designs the system to motivate subordinates to perform in a desired fashion, to do what they would not do if left to their own devices.

Timing

In any performance measurement system the timing of the measure should fit the task at hand (Lawler and Rhode, 1976). The timing of the measure can influence the output. For example, if performance on a ten-year project is measured annually, annual products will result, which may or may not be meaningful to long-run performance. In a ten-year project there will probably be intermediate results produced before the end of the project, but there is no reason to believe that results necessarily occur annually. If the project takes less than a year, the generation of results will be within the evaluation cycle. However, for projects that run longer than a year, annual evaluations will produce results simply because the results are required, probably as inputs to the annual budget cycle. The budget tends to be a major control device within the management control system. The budget not only is a financial plan that sets forth fiscal goals within an organization but also acts as a device for motivation, planning, and control (Kenis, 1979).

Historically, the problem of performing accounting evaluations of research and development operations is just such a problem (Hayes, 1977)—although it is less a problem now because of changes in accounting standards. What are the financial measures of progress from the inception of an idea to the finished product? The final outputs of research—the results— are easy to measure. However, timing can be a problem. Managers, stockholders, and bankers require regularly scheduled financial reports. Therefore numbers are needed that match the accounting period. When people do basic research, they cannot say, "Hmmm, two weeks left in the accounting period; I had better make a discovery." Research does not work that way. It becomes very difficult for the financial system to deal with the R&D process. The same problem occurs almost anytime a service or creative process is involved. What is the measure of output of an attorney's office—pages of briefs filed?

One obvious solution to the timing issue is to put individuals on an evaluation schedule that matches the normal production cycle. Current assets at a Scotch whiskey distillery are on a twelve-year cycle. At first glance this may solve the problem of the arbitrary segmentation of a service or creative process. On the other hand, how is the financial reporting of the service or creative process under the new system to be integrated with the other parts of the organization? This is not always clear.

Bottom up and top down

Should the impetus for the design of a management control system come from the top or from the bottom of the organization? The impetus and design of the system should be top down *and* bottom up. Cooper, Hayes, and Wolf (1981) cite an example presented by Lidowsky of employees meticulously following a system they did not accept. Eventually the employees swamped the system. Subordinates who do not accept a management control system can destroy it. Commitment must exist at all levels, or the system is not going to work.

Outside support

Is there support from the outside the organization for the management control system? In the federal government, support from the Office of Management and Budget or the General Accounting Office for a particular management control system may cause that system to prevail over other competing systems. In the private sector the management control system likely to succeed is the one that will facilitate the organization's dealings with its customers and suppliers. If for no other reason, commitment and support will probably be gained from those people who deal with the other organizations.

The designers

A management control system should be designed by a mix of individuals who have abilities in accounting, organizational analysis, and management information design and who are sensitive to the planning cycle. A system designed solely by financial accountants will probably have a strong financial accounting or fiduciary emphasis, which may not be what is needed for management control purposes. There is a difference between fiduciary control and management control. Fiduciary control is concerned that the money be spent legally, according to the rules. Management control is concerned that resources are used in a way that most efficiently and effectively helps meet organizational goals.

Boland (1981) compares the thinking of Argyris and Churchman on the design of systems. Argyris argues that the only way to acquire sufficient knowledge to make design judgments in a meaningful way is to be aware of how the people within the organization behave. The way to gain that knowledge is to become part of the organization. In contrast, Churchman contends that the designer should stand back and take a "macro" look at the system to be designed. The designer should not become involved in the organization, keeping individual bias out of the design process so judgments can be objective. He believes that personal involvement may cause the designer to lose perspective; the designer cannot make critical judgments, such as what should and should not be measured. As Boland points out, the designer needs to be both:

1. part of the system, involved enough to understand the informal things that are going on and, to some extent, the personalities of the individuals involved; and
2. able to step back and make the judgments.

If a consultant is used, the consultant's rewards must be contingent on successful implementation of the system and not just on the design of the system.

Line versus staff needs

As a group of experts in a particular area the staff tends to ask for a particular kind of information. The data requested by staff are probably generated by the management control system and therefore collected by the line personnel. If the function of staff is to support the line personnel, the staff should not hinder the line, such as by demanding that line personnel gather additional information. It is questionable whether staff or support individuals need to have information other than what the line personnel use. While some argue that the staff people need unique kinds of information, it is likely that staff can extrapolate this information from data already available.

External reporting needs

Both private- and public-sector organizations must develop information necessary for external reporting. Operating parallel accounting systems—one for internal reporting, another for external reporting—will probably not be efficient. Therefore, a private-sector company developing its management control system will probably ensure that the cost accounting information be part of that system and that it can be used for external reporting purposes. For public-sector organizations, operating data will be needed to run the organization, but the external funding source may ask for a different set of data. To minimize the cost of reporting, the use of statistical cost data should be considered. Though perhaps not desirable for operating information, statistical cost data may be perfectly appropriate for outside reporting (Anthony and Herzlinger, 1980).

Resistance

Change is disruptive. Any new management control system represents change to those who will be affected by the system. If the individuals perceive the system as a threat to their well-being and security, they will probably resist it. Well-being and security can broadly be defined as maintaining one's place in the power structure and status relationships in the organization. The control system can threaten well-being and security in a number of ways. One way is by automating jobs, thus rendering selective individual expertise unnecessary. Possible areas of automation would be purchasing, historical data analysis, and report generation. Inasmuch as the new management control system is able to measure performance and behavior of individuals more accurately, the individuals being measured may feel threatened because they will be more closely observed and a possible loss of freedom may result. Additionally, a new management control system will probably create new centers of power because new people will be experts in regard to the particular system. With any system, some will gain and some will lose (Lawler and Rhode, 1976).

THE MANAGEMENT CONTROL SYSTEM AND THE OPERATING ENVIRONMENT

A well-designed control system is not necessarily transferable from one environment to another. A system designed to operate in a stable environment with a stable technology is not necessarily going to work when placed in an unstable environment with changing technology.

Dirsmith and Jablonsky (1979) have shown that a system such as zero-base budgeting (ZBB) that was designed for one environment, performed differently when moved to another environment. ZBB provided Texas Instruments a vehicle in an uncertain, dynamic environment. Flexibility was given to the local manager to have funds to meet goals and objectives. ZBB was developed for the manager in a loosely coupled organization. In the federal government ZBB was a paper-intensive system by which individuals documented exactly what they were doing and verified that they were not spending money illegally. ZBB in essence had two faces, one for industry (Texas Instruments) as a means to operate in a highly dynamic environment and one for the federal government as a method for documenting stability. A management control system that works in one organization is not necessarily going to work in another since the environment, labor force, culture, and other factors that affect the management control system may be different.

SUMMARY

The segregation of planning, control, and evaluation into separate chapters was useful for pedagogical purposes, but in practice these functions cannot be separated. You plan in order to know where you are going; you control so you can get there; and you evaluate in order to know whether you have arrived. The topics of the various chapters are all interrelated. Each of the processes in the management control system is built on incomplete theory. There is thus no guarantee that the system will work until it is implemented. If it works, fine. If it does not work, the information it generates may still help to explicate the theory of management control systems.

SUGGESTED READINGS

Ansari, Shahid L. An integrated approach to control system design. *Accounting, Organizations, and Society,* 1977, *2*(2), 101-112.

Boland, Richard J., Jr. A study in system design: C. West Churchman and Chris Argyris. *Accounting, Organizations, and Society,* 1981, *6*(2), 109-118.

Cammann, Cortland. Effects of the use of control systems. *Accounting, Organizations, and Society,* 1976, *1*(4), 301-313.

Hofstede, Geert. Management control of public and not-for-profit activities. *Accounting, Organizations, and Society,* 1981, *6*(3), 193-211.

Lawrence, Paul R. and Jay W. Lorsch. *Organization and Environment.* Cambridge: Harvard University Press, 1979.

Ouchi, William G. A conceptual framework for the design of organizational control mechanisms. *Management Science,* September 1979, *25*(9), 833-848.

BIBLIOGRAPHY

Abert, James G. and Murray Kamrass (Eds.). *Social Experiments and Social Program Evaluation*. Cambridge: Ballinger Publishing Company, 1974.

Ackoff, Russel L. *A Concept of Corporate Planning*. New York: Wiley-Interscience, 1970.

Adler, Lee. Time lag in new product development. *Journal of Marketing*, January 1966, *30* (1), 17-21.

American Accounting Association. Report of Committee on Internal Measurement and Reporting. *The Accounting Review, Supplement*, 1973, *48*, 208-223.

American Accounting Association. Report of the Committee on Accounting Theory Construction and Verification. *The Accounting Review, Supplement*, 1971, *46*, 50-79.

American Accounting Association. Report of Committee on Managerial Decision Models. *The Accounting Review, Supplement*, 1969, *44*, 42-76.

Amey, Lloyd R. *Budget Planning and Control Systems*. London: Pitman Publishing, 1979.

Anderson, Scarvia B. and Samuel Ball. *The Profession and Practice of Program Evaluation*. San Francisco: Jossey-Bass Publishers, 1978.

Ansari, Shahid L. An integrated approach to control system design. *Accounting, Organizations, and Society*, 1977, *2*(2), 101-112.

Anthony, Robert N. *Planning and Control Systems: A Framework for Analysis*. Boston: Harvard University, 1965.

Anthony, Robert N. and John Dearden. *Management Control Systems* (4th Edition). Homewood, Ill.: Richard D. Irwin, 1980.

Anthony, R. N. and R. E. Herzlinger, *Management Control in NonProfit Organizations* (Revised Edition). Homewood, Ill.: Richard D. Irwin, 1980.

Bibliography

Ashby, W. Ross. Principles of the self-organizing system. In Heinz von Foerster and George W. Zopf (Eds.). *Principles of Self-Organization.* New York: Pergamon Press, 1962, pp. 255-278.

Ashton, Robert H. Deviation-amplifying feedback and unintended consequences of management accounting systems. *Accounting, Organizations and Society,* 1976, *1*(4), 289-300.

Attkisson, C. Clifford and Anthony Broskowski. Evaluation and the emerging human service concept. In C. Clifford Attkisson, William A. Hargreaves, Mardi J. Horowitz, and James E. Sorensen (Eds.)., *Evaluation of Human Service Programs.* New York: Academic Press, 1978, pp. 4-7.

Baker, Frank (Ed.). *Organizational Systems: General Systems Approach to Complex Organizations.* Homewood, Ill.: Richard D. Irwin, 1973.

Beckhard, Richard and Reuben Harris. *Organizational Transitions: Managing Complex Change.* Reading, Mass.: Addison-Wesley Publishing Company, 1977.

Beer, Stafford. *Cybernetics and Management.* New York: John Wiley & Sons, 1964.

Berrien, F. Kenneth. *General and Social Systems.* New Brunswick, N.J.: Rutgers University Press, 1968.

Bertalanffy, Ludwig Von. General systems theory—A critical review. *General Systems,* 1962, *7,* 1-20.

Bertalanffy, Ludwig Von. *General System Theory: Foundations, Development, Applications.* New York: George Braziller, 1968.

Blau, Peter M. *Bureaucracy in Modern Society.* New York: Random House, 1956.

Blau, Peter M. and Richard A. Schoenherr. *The Structure of Organizations.* New York: Basic Books, 1971.

Boland, Richard J., Jr. A Study in system design: C. West Churchman and Chris Argyris. *Accounting, Organizations and Society,* 1981, *6*(2), 109-118.

Boulding, Kenneth E. General systems theory—The skeleton of science. *Management Science,* 1956, *2,* 197-208.

Bower, J. I. *Managing the Resource Allocation Process: A Study of Corporate Planning and Investment.* Boston: Division of Research, Graduate School of Business Administration, Harvard University, 1970.

Box, George E. P. Evolutionary operation: A method for increasing industrial productivity. *Applied Statistics,* June 1957, *6*(2), 81-101.

Brace, Paul K., Robert Elkin, Daniel D. Robinson, and Harold I. Steinberg. *Reporting of Service Efforts and Accomplishments.* Stamford, Conn.: Financial Accounting Standards Board, 1980.

Bracker, J. The Historical Development of the Strategic Management Process. *Academy of Management Review,* April 1980, *5*(2), 219–224.

Brillouin, L. Life, thermodynamics, and cybernetics. In Walter Buckley (Ed.), *Modern Systems Research for the Behavioral Scientist.* Chicago: Aldine Publishing Company, 1968, pp. 147–156.

Brillouin, I. Thermodynamics and information theory. *American Scientist,* October 1950, *38,* 594–599.

Bromiley, Philip and K. J. Euske. The Use of Rational Systems in Bounded Rationality Organizations: A Scilla and Charybdis for the Financial Manager. Unpublished manuscript, Naval Postgraduate School, February 9, 1983.

Bruns, William J., Jr. and Don T. DeCoster. *Accounting and Its Behavioral Implications.* New York: McGraw-Hill Book Company, 1969.

Buckley, Walter. A systems model of societal regulation. In Arlyn J. Melcher (Ed.). *General Systems and Organization Theory: Methodological Aspects.* Kent, Ohio: Kent State University Press, 1975, 17–21.

Buckley, Walter (Ed.). *Modern Systems Research for the Behavioral Scientist.* Chicago: Aldine Publishing Company, 1968.

Camilles, John C. and John H. Grant. Operational planning: The integration of programming and budgeting. *Academy of Management Review,* July 1980, *5*(3), pp. 369–379.

Cammann, Cortland. Effects of the use of control systems. *Accounting, Organizations and Society,* 1976, *1*(4), 301–313.

Cannon, Walter B. Self-regulation of the body. The wisdom of the body. In Walter Buckley (Ed.). *Modern Systems Research for the Behavioral Scientist.* Chicago: Aldine Publishing Company, 1968, pp. 256–258.

Carnap, Rudolf. Foundations of logic and mathematics. In Otto Neurath, Rudolf Carnap, and Charles Morris (Eds.). *International Encyclopedia of Unified Science,* Vol. 1, No. 3. Chicago: University of Chicago Press, 1955, pp. 42–62.

Churchman, C. West. *The Systems Approach.* New York: Dell Publishing Company, 1968.

Churchman, C. West. Why measure? In C. West Churchman and Philburn Ratoosh (Eds.). *Measurement Definitions and Theories.* New York: John Wiley & Sons, 1962, pp. 83–94.

Churchman, C. West. *Prediction and Optimal Decision.* Englewood Cliffs, N.J.: Prentice-Hall, 1961.

Cohen, Michael D., James G. March, and Johan P. Olsen. People, Problems, Solutions, and the Ambiguity of Relevance. In James G. March, and Johan P. Olsen (Eds.). *Ambiguity and Choice in Organizations.* Bergen, Norway: Universitetsforlaget, 1976, pp. 24–37.

Cohen, Morris R. and Ernest Nagel. *An Introduction to Logic and Scientific Method.* London: Routledge & Kegan Paul, 1934.

Cooper, David J., David Hayes, and Frank Wolf. Accounting in organized anarchies: Understanding and designing accounting systems in ambiguous situations. *Accounting, Organizations and Society,* 1981, 6(3), 175-191.

Crawford, C. Merle. Marketing research and the new product failure rate. *Journal of Marketing,* April 1977, 41(2), 51-61.

Cummings, Thomas G. *Systems Theory for Organization Development.* Chichester, England: John Wiley & Sons, Ltd., 1980.

Cyert, Richard M. and James G. March. *A Behavioral Theory of the Firm.* Englewood Cliffs, N.J.: Prentice-Hall, 1963.

Dalton, Gene W. Motivation and control in organizations. In Gene W. Dalton, and Paul R. Lawrence (Eds.). *Motivation and Control in Organizations.* Homewood, Ill.: Richard D. Irwin, 1971, pp. 1-35.

Dalton, Gene W. and Paul R. Lawrence. *Motivation and Control in Organizations.* Homewood, Ill.: Richard D. Irwin, 1971.

Demski, Joel. Uncertainty and evaluation based on controllable performance. *Journal of Accounting Research,* Autumn 1976, 14(2), 230-245.

Dermer, Jerry. *Management Planning and Control Systems.* Homewood, Ill.: Richard D. Irwin, 1977.

Devine, Carl Thomas. Some conceptual problems in accounting measurements. In Robert K. Jaedicke, Yuji Ijiri, and Oswald Nielsen (Eds.). *Research in Accounting Measurement: Collected Papers.* Sarasota: Fla. American Accounting Association, 1966, pp. 13-27.

Dewey, John. *How We Think.* Boston: D. C. Heath, 1910.

Dirsmith, Mark W. and Stephen F. Jablonsky. Zero-base budgeting as a management technique and political strategy. *Academy of Management Review.* October 1979, 4(4), 555-565.

Drucker, Peter F. *The Practice of Management.* New York: Harper & Row, 1954.

Emery, James C. *Organizational Planning and Control Systems.* London: MacMillan Company, 1969.

Euske, K. J., D. W. Jackson, and W. E. Reif. Performance and satisfaction of bank managers. *Journal of Bank Research,* Spring 1980, 11(1), 36-42.

Ferrara, William L. Responsibility accounting—A basic control concept. *National Association of Accountants Bulletin,* September 1964.

Forrester, J. W. Managerial decision making. In Martin Greenberger (Ed.). *Management and the Computer of the Future.* Boston: MIT Press, 1962, pp. 37-68.

Fremgen, James N. *Accounting for Managerial Analysis* (3rd Edition.) Homewood, Ill.: Richard D. Irwin, 1976.

Friedman, Milton. *Capitalism and Freedom.* Chicago: University of Chicago Press, 1962.

Gerboth, Dale I. Research, intuition, and politics in accounting inquiry. *The Accounting Review,* July 1973, *48*(3), 475–482.

Gershefski, George W. Building a corporate financial model. *Harvard Business Review,* July–August 1969, pp. 61–72.

Goodman, Paul S., Johannes M. Pennings, and associates. *New Perspectives on Organizational Effectiveness.* San Francisco: Jossey-Bass, 1979.

Gordon, Lawrence A., Danny Miller, and Henry Mintzberg. *Normative Models in Managerial Decision-Making.* New York: National Association of Accountants, 1975.

Gouldner, Alvin W. *Patterns of Industrial Bureaucracy.* New York: Free Press, 1954.

Hall, A. D. and F. E. Fagen. Definition of system. *General Systems,* 1956, *1*, 18–28.

Hall, Francine S. Organization goals: The status of theory and research. In J. Leslie Livingstone (Ed.). *Managerial Accounting: The Behavioral Foundations.* Columbus, Ohio: Grid, 1975, pp. 9–32.

Hamblin, A. C. *Evaluation and Control of Training.* London: McGraw-Hill Book Company, 1974.

Hardin, Garrett. The cybernetics of competition: A biologist's view of society. In Walter Buckley (Ed.). *Modern Systems Research for the Behavioral Scientist.* Chicago: Aldine Publishing Company, 1968, pp. 449–459.

Hargreaves, William A. and C. Clifford Attkisson. Evaluating program outcomes. In C. Clifford Attkisson, William A. Hargreaves, and James E. Sorensen (Eds.). *Evaluation of Human Service Programs.* New York: Academic Press, 1978, pp. 303–339.

Hayes, David C. The contingency theory of managerial accounting: A reply. *The Accounting Review,* April 1978, *53*(2), 530–532.

Hayes, David C. The contingency theory of managerial accounting. *The Accounting Review,* January 1977, *52*(1), 22–39.

Hayes, Robert H. and William J. Abernathy. Managing our way to economic decline. *Harvard Business Review,* July–August 1980, pp. 68–77.

Hill, Walter. The goal formation process in complex organizations. *Journal of Management Studies,* 1969, *6*(2), 198–208.

Hofstede, Geert. Management control of public and not-for-profit activities. *Accounting, Organizations and Society,* 1981, *6*(3), 193–211.

Hofstede, G. B. The game of budget control. In Robert N. Anthony, John Dearden, and Richard F. Vancil (Eds.). *Management Control Systems.* Homewood, Ill.: Richard D. Irwin, 1980.

Holzer, H. Peter (Ed.). *Management Accounting 1980: Proceedings of the University of Illinois Management Accounting Symposium.* Urbana-Champaign:University of Illinois, 1980.

Hopwood, Anthony. *Accounting and Human Behavior.* Englewood Cliffs, N.J.: Prentice-Hall, 1974.

Horngren, Charles T. *Cost Accounting: A Managerial Emphasis* (5th Edition). Englewood Cliffs, N.J.: Prentice-Hall, 1982.

Hovland, Carl I., Irving I. Janis, and Harold H. Kelley. *Communication and Persuasion.* New Haven, Conn.: Yale University Press, 1968.

Ijiri, Yuji. *Studies in Accounting Research, No. 10: Theory of Accounting Measurement.* Sarasota, Fla: American Accounting Association, 1975.

Ijiri, Yuji. *The Foundations of Accounting Measurement.* Englewood Cliffs, N.J.: Prentice-Hall, 1967.

Ijiri, Yuji, Robert K. Jaedicke, and Kenneth E. Knight. The Effects of accounting alternatives on management decisions. In Robert K. Jaedicke, Yuji Ijiri, and Oswald Nielsen (Eds.), *Research in Accounting Measurement: Collected Papers.* Sarasota, Fla: American Accounting Association, 1966, pp. 186–199.

Ijiri, Yuji, Robert K. Jaedicke, and Oswald Nielsen (Eds.). *Research in Accounting Measurement.* Menasha, Wisc.: George Banta Company, 1966.

Kast, Fremont E. and James E. Rosenzweig. General systems theory: Applications for organization and management. *Academy of Management Journal,* December 1972, *15*(4), 447–465.

Kenis, Izzettin. Effects of budgetary goal characteristics on managerial attitudes and performance. *The Accounting Review,* October 1979, *54*(4), 707–721.

Kepner, Charles H. and Benjamin E. Tregoe. *The Rational Manager.* New York: McGraw-Hill Book Company, 1965.

Kerr, Steven. On the folly of rewarding A, while hoping for B. *Academy of Management Journal,* December 1975, *18*(4), 769–783.

Kerr, Steven and John W. Slocum Jr. Controlling the performance of people in organizations. In Paul C. Nystrom and William H. Starbuck (Eds.), *Handbook of Organizational Design, Volume 2, Remodeling Organizations and Their Environments.* Oxford: Oxford University Press, 1981, pp. 116–134.

Kohler, Eric I. *A Dictionary for Accountants* (5th Edition). Englewood Cliffs, N.J.: Prentice-Hall, 1975.

Koontz, Harold and Robert W. Bradspies. Managing through feedforward control. *Business Horizons,* June 1972, *4*(3), 25-36.

Kremyanskiy, V. I. Certain peculiarities of organisms as a "system" from the point of view of physics, cybernetics, and biology. In Walter Buckley (Ed.). *Modern Systems Research for the Behavioral Scientist.* Chicago: Aldine Publishing Company, 1968.

Kuhn, Thomas S. *The Structure of Scientific Revolutions* (2nd Edition). In Otto Neurath (Ed.). *International Encyclopedia of Unified Science,* Vol. 2, No. 2. Chicago: University of Chicago Press, 1970.

Lawler, Edward E., III, and John Grant Rhode. *Information and Control in Organizations.* Pacific Palisades, Calif.: Goodyear Publishing Company, 1976.

Lawrence, Paul R. and Jay W. Lorsch. *Organization and Environment.* Cambridge: Harvard University Press, 1979.

Lawrence, Paul R. and Jay W. Lorsch. *Studies in Organizational Design.* Homewood, Ill.: Richard D. Irwin, 1970.

Lebas, Michel. Toward a theory of management control: Organizational, information economics, and behavioral approaches. Unpublished manuscript, Centre d'Enseignement Superieur des Affaires, Jouy en Josas, France, September 1980.

Le Breton, Preston P. *General Administration: Planning and Implementation.* New York: Holt, Rinehart & Winston, 1965.

Levitan, Sar A. and Gregory K. Wurzburg. *Evaluating Federal Social Programs: An Uncertain Art.* Kalamazoo, Mich.: Upjohn Institute for Employment Research, 1979.

Lightman, Alan. Science on the Right Side of the Brain. *Science 82,* July-August 1982, *3*(5), 28, 30.

Livingstone, J. Leslie. *Managerial Accounting: The Behavioral Foundations.* Columbus, Ohio: Grid, 1975*a*.

Livingstone, J. Leslie. Organizational goals and the budget process. In J. Leslie Livingstone (Ed.). *Managerial Accounting: The Behavioral Foundations.* Columbus, Ohio: Grid, 1975*b*, 33-47.

Lorange, Peter. *Corporate Planning: An Executive Viewpoint.* Englewood Cliffs, N.J.: Prentice-Hall, 1980.

Loving, Rush, Jr. The Penn Central Bankruptcy Express. *Fortune,* August 1970, pp. 104-109, 164-166, 171.

Lynn, E. S. and R. J. Freeman. *Fund Accounting: Theory and Practice.* Englewood Cliffs, N.J.: Prentice-Hall, 1974.

Lynn, Laurence E., Jr. (Ed.). *Studies in the Management of Social R&D: Selected Policy Areas.* Washington, D.C.: National Academy of Sciences, 1979.

Maciariello, Joseph A. *Program-Management Control Systems.* New York: John Wiley & Sons, 1978.

March, James G. The technology of foolishness. In James G. March and Johan P. Olsen (Eds.). *Ambiguity and Choice in Organizations.* Bergen, Norway: Universitetsforlaget, 1976, 69–81.

March, James G. and Johan P. Olsen. Organizational choice under ambiguity. In James G. March and Johan P. Olsen (Eds.). *Ambiguity and Choice in Organizations.* Bergen, Norway: Universitetsforlaget, 1976, 10–23.

March, James G. and Herbert A. Simon. *Organizations.* New York: John Wiley & Sons, 1958.

Margenau, Henry. *The Nature of Physical Reality.* New York: McGraw-Hill Book Company, 1950.

Mattessich, Richard. *Instrumental Reasoning and Systems Methodology.* Dordrecht, Holland: D. Reidel Publishing Company, 1978.

Melcher, Arlyn J. (Ed.). *General Systems and Organization Theory: Methodological Aspects.* Kent, Ohio: Kent State University Press, 1975.

Merton, Robert K. Bureaucratic structure and personality. *Social Forces,* May 1940, *18,* 560–568.

Milani, Ken. The relationship of participation in budget setting to industrial supervisor performance and attitudes: A field study. *Accounting Review,* April 1975, *50*(2), 274–284.

Miller, E. J. and A. K. Rice. *Systems of Organization.* London: Tavistock Publications, 1967.

Miller, James G. The nature of living systems. *Behavioral Science,* July 1971, *16,* 278–301.

Mintzberg, Henry. *Impediments to the Use of Management Information.* New York: National Association of Accountants, 1975.

Mize, Joe H., Charles R. White, and George H. Brooks. *Operations Planning and Control.* Englewood Cliffs, N.J.: Prentice-Hall, 1971.

Mock, Theodore J. and Hugh D. Grove. *Measurement Accounting and Information.* New York: John Wiley & Sons, 1979.

Newman, William H. *Constructive Control: Design and Use of Control Systems.* Englewood Cliffs, N.J.: Prentice-Hall, 1975.

Newman, William H. *Administrative Action.* Englewood Cliffs, N.J.: Prentice-Hall, 1951.

Nove, Alec. *The Soviet Economic System.* London: George Allen and Unwin, 1977.

Odiorne, George. *Management by Objectives.* New York: Pittman Publishing Company, 1965.

Ouchi, William G. A conceptual framework for the design of organizational control mechanisms. *Management Science,* September 1979, 25(9), 833–848.

Pattillo, James W. *Zero-base Budgeting: A Planning, Resource Allocation, and Control Tool.* New York: National Association of Accountants, 1977.

Perrow, Charles. The analysis of goals in complex organizations. *American Sociological Review,* 1961, 26, 854–866.

Pfeffer, Jeffrey and Gerald R. Salancik. *The External Control of Organizations: A Resource Dependence Perspective.* New York: Harper & Row, 1978.

Popper, Karl R. *Objective Knowledge.* Oxford, England: Oxford University Press, 1972.

Phyrr, P. A. *Zero-Based Budgeting: A Practical Management Tool for Evaluating Expense.* New York: John Wiley & Sons, 1973.

Rappaport, Alfred. "A fatal fascination with the short run. *Business Week,* May 4, 1981, pp. 20–21.

Raymond, Richard C. Communication, entropy, and life. In Walter Buckley (Ed.), *Modern Systems Research for the Behavioral Scientist.* Chicago: Aldine Publishing Company, 1968.

Ridgway, V. F. Dysfunctional consequences of performance measurement. *Administrative Science Quarterly,* September 1956, 1(2), 240–247.

Ronen, Joshua. Budgets as tools of control and motivation. In J. Leslie Livingstone (Ed.). *Managerial Accounting: The Behavioral Foundations.* Columbus, Ohio: Grid, 1975, pp. 157–165.

Ronen, J. and J. L. Livingstone. An expectancy theory approach to the motivational impacts of budgets. *The Accounting Review,* October 1975, 50(4), 671–685.

Rosen, Robert. *Fundamentals of Measurement and Representation of Natural Systems.* New York: Elsevier North-Holland, 1978.

Rosenblueth, Arturo, Norbert Wiener, and Julian Bigelow. Behavior, purpose, and Teleology. In Walter Buckley (Ed.). *Modern Systems Research for the Behavioral Scientist.* Chicago: Aldine Publishing Company, 1968, pp. 221–225.

Rossi, Peter H., Howard E. Freeman, and Sonia R. Wright. *Evaluation: A Systematic Approach.* Beverly Hills, Calif.: Sage Publications, 1979.

Rossi, Peter H. and Walter Williams (Eds.). *Evaluating Social Programs.* New York: Seminar Press, 1972.

Rothman, Jack. *Social R&D: Research and Development in the Human Services.* Englewood Cliffs, N.J.: Prentice-Hall, 1980.

Rudner, Richard S. *Philosophy of Social Science.* Englewood Cliffs, N.J.: Prentice-Hall, 1966.

Schiff, Michael and Arie Y. Lewin. *Behavioral Aspects of Accounting.* Englewood Cliffs, N.J.: Prentice-Hall, 1974.

Schrader, William J. and Robert E. Malcom. A note on accounting theory construction and verification. *Abacus,* June 1973, *9,* 93-98.

Schrodinger, Erwin. Order, disorder, and entropy. What is life? In Walter Buckley (Ed.). *Modern Systems Research for the Behavioral Scientist.* Chicago: Aldine Publishing Company, 1968, pp. 143-146.

Selznick, P. *TVA and the Grass Roots.* Berkeley: University of California Press, 1949.

Shillinglaw, Gordon. *Managerial Cost Accounting* (4th Edition). Homeward, Ill.: Richard D. Irwin, 1977.

Simon, Herbert. On the concept of organization goal. *Administrative Science Quarterly,* June 1964, *9*(1), 1-22.

Skinner, B. F. *Reflections on Behaviorism and Society.* Englewood Cliffs, N.J.: Prentice-Hall, 1978.

Steiner, George A. *Top Management Planning.* London: MacMillan Company, 1969.

Steiner, George A. (Ed.). *Managerial Long-Range Planning.* New York: McGraw-Hill Book Company, 1963.

Sterling, Robert R. On theory construction and verification. *The Accounting Review,* July 1970, *45*(3), 444-457.

Stevens, S. S. On the theory of scales of measurement. *Science,* June 1946, *103*(2685), 677-680.

Stufflebeam, Daniel L., Walter J. Foley, William J. Gephart, Egon G. Guba, Raymond L. Hammond, Howard O. Merriman, and Malcom M. Provus. *Educational Evaluation and Decision Making.* Itasca, Ill.: F. E. Peacock Publishers, 1971.

Suchman, Edward A. *Evaluative Research.* New York: Russell Sage Foundation, 1967.

Swieringa, Robert J. and Robert H. Moncur. *Some Effects of Participative Budgeting on Managerial Behavior.* New York: National Association of Accountants, 1975.

Swinth, Robert L. Organizational planning: Goal setting in interdependent systems. *Industrial Management Review,* 1966, *7,* 57-70.

Thomas, Arthur L. *A Behavioral Analysis of Joint-Cost and Transfer Pricing.* Champaign, Ill.: Stipes Publishing Company, 1980.

Thomas, Arthur L. Evaluating the effectiveness of social programs. *Journal of Accountancy,* June 1976, pp. 65-71.

Thompson, James D. *Organizations in Action.* New York: McGraw-Hill Book Company, 1967.
Tiessen, Peter and J. H. Waterhouse. The contingency theory of managerial accounting: A comment. *Accounting Review,* April 1978, *53*(2), 523-529.
Torgerson, Warren S. *Theory and Methods of Scaling.* New York: John Wiley & Sons, 1967.
Tosi, Henry. The human effects of managerial budgeting systems. In J. Leslie Livingstone (Ed.). *Managerial Accounting: The Behavioral Foundations.* Columbus, Ohio: Grid, 1975, pp. 139-156.
Vancil, Richard F. *Decentralization: Managerial Ambiguity by Design.* Homewood, Ill.: Dow Jones-Irwin, 1979.
Waterhouse, J. H. and P. Tiessen. A contingency framework for management accounting systems research. *Accounting, Organizations, and Society,* 1978, *3*(1), 65-76.
Watson, David J. H. and John V. Baumler. Transfer pricing: A behavioral context. *The Accounting Review,* July 1975, *50*(3), 466-474.
Weick, Karl E. *The Psychology of Organizing.* Reading, Mass.: Addison-Wesley Publishing Company, 1969.
Weiss, Carol H. *Evaluating Action Programs: Readings in Social Action and Education.* Boston: Allyn and Bacon, 1972*a*.
Weiss, Carol H. *Evaluation Research: Methods for Assessing Program Effectiveness.* Englewood Cliffs, N.J.: Prentice-Hall, 1972*b*.
Wholey, Joseph S. *Evaluation: Promise and Performance.* Washington, D.C.: Urban Institute, 1979.
Williams, Thomas H. and Charles H. Griffin. On the nature of empirical verification in accounting. *Abacus,* December 1969, pp. 143-78.
Wilson, R.M.S. *Management Controls and Marketing Planning.* London: Heinemann, 1980.

AUTHOR INDEX

Abernathy, William J., 49
Ackoff, Russel L., 15, 16, 17, 18, 19, 21, 23, 25, 26, 32, 38, 41-42, 43
Adler, Lee, 15
American Accounting Association, 100-101, 104-105, 106, 107
Amey, Lloyd R., 33, 35, 36
Ansari, Shahid L., 5, 33, 111
Anthony, Robert N., 2, 5, 22, 23, 48, 110, 118
Argyris, Chris, 117
Ashton, Robert H., 45
Attkisson, C. Clifford, 60-63

Beckhard, Richard, 25
Blau, Peter M., 64
Boland, Richard J., Jr., 117
Boulding, Kenneth E., 10
Box, George E. P., 29-30
Brace, Paul K., 5
Bracker, J., 22
Bradspies, Robert W. 33, 35
Bromiley, Philip, 7
Broskowski, Anthony, 60-63

Carnap, Rudolf, 97

Churchman, C. West, 77, 78, 83-84, 85, 86, 91, 117
Cohen, Morris R., 104-105
Cooper, David J., 113, 114, 116
Crawford, C. Merle, 15
Cyert, Richard M., 28

Dalton, Gene W., 32, 33, 36, 45, 48, 50
Dearden, John, 23
Demski, Joel, 38-39
Dewey, John, 22
Dirsmith, Mark W., 119
Drucker, Peter F., 112

Emery, James C., 15, 17, 18, 19-21, 30
Euske, K. J., 7, 71

Fagin, F. E., 10
Forrester, J. W., 106
Freeman, R. J., 21
Fremgen, James N., 21
Friedman, Milton, 48

Gerboth, Dale I., 102-103
Gouldner, Alvin W., 45-46

133

Author Index

Griffin, Charles H., 104
Grove, Hugh D., 78, 81, 82-83, 86, 87-89

Hall, A. D., 10
Hall, Francine S., 27, 28-29
Hardin, Garrett, 10, 23-26
Harris, Reuben, 25
Hayes, David, 49, 113, 114, 115, 116
Herzlinger, R. E., 22, 48, 118
Hill, Walter, 29
Hofstede, Geert, 2, 110, 112
Hopwood, Anthony, 33, 36, 56, 57, 71-72
Horngren, Charles T., 21

Ijiri, Yuji, 84, 86, 89

Jablonsky, Stephen F., 119
Jaedicke, Robert K., 84, 86, 89

Kast, Fremont E., 10
Kenis, Izzettin, 112, 115
Kerr, Steven, 9, 47, 112
Knight, Kenneth E., 84, 86, 89
Koontz, Harold, 33, 35
Kuhn, Thomas S., 6

Lawler, Edward E., III, 48, 111, 112, 113, 115, 118
Lebas, Michel, 5
Lightman, Alan, 105
Lynn, E. S., 21

March, James G., 17, 28, 114
Margenau, Henry, 77
Merton, Robert K., 45, 46
Milani, Ken, 112
Mock, Theodore J., 78, 81, 82-83, 86, 87-89
Moncur, Robert H., 112

Nagel, Ernest, 104-105
Newman, William H., 15, 32, 33-35, 36, 38, 39-43, 46-47, 48, 49-50, 67
Nove, Alec, 9

Odiorne, George, 112

Perrow, Charles, 27, 29
Phyrr, P. A., 21

Rappaport, Alfred, 7, 49, 73
Rhode, John Grant, 48, 111, 112, 113, 115, 118
Ridgway, V. F., 40, 48
Rosenzweig, James E., 10
Rudner, Richard S., 76, 95, 99, 104

Selznick, P., 45, 46
Shillinglaw, Gordon, 21
Simon, Herbert, 17, 28
Skinner, B. F., 96
Slocum, John W., 112
Steiner, George A., 19
Sterling, Robert R., 97, 98, 99-100
Stevens, S. S., 77, 78, 79, 87
Stufflebeam, Daniel, 53-56, 58-60, 65-67, 68
Suchman, Edward A., 60, 64-65, 68
Swieringa, Robert J., 112

Thomas, Arthur L., 71
Thompson, James D., 27, 29
Torgerson, Warren S. 76, 77, 78-79, 87, 96, 97, 102
Tosi, Henry, 114

Weick, Karl E., 25, 113
Weiss, Carol H., 68-69
Williams, Thomas H., 104
Wolf, Frank, 113, 114, 116

SUBJECT INDEX

Actual effects, 5, 6
Analytical schema, 76
Attributes measured. *See*
    Performance measures
Axiomatic system, 95-101

Causal factors, 5, 6
Components of a management
    control system, 3
Composite feedback, 40
Control, 5-7, 32-50, 101, 110
    achieving, 48-50
    administrative, 36
    adapter, 35
    behavioral models of, 33
    compensatory, 35
    contrasted to planning, 18, 21
    defined, 32, 33
    feedback, 35
    feedforward, 35
    group, 36
    individual, 36
    learning, 35
    limits, 40
    organizational, 36
    paradox of, 45-48
    postaction, 33-35
    process, 36-43
    reaction to, 45-48
    reciprocity of, 43, 44
    self, 36
    social, 36
    steering, 33-35
    structural models of, 33
    unintended consequences of,
        45-48
    yes-no, 33-35
Corporate advertising, 57

Design considerations, 111-118
Desired effects, 5, 6

Empirical sciences, 99-101
Equifinality, 106
Evaluation, 5, 7, 53, 101, 110
    definitions, 53-60
        congruence, 54
        judgment, 58
        measurement, 53
    purposes of, 68, 69
    related to control, 71-73
    types of, 60-68
        adequacy, 62, 64
        context, 67
        effectiveness, 61, 64
        efficiency, 62, 65
        effort, 61, 64
        input, 67

Subject Index

process, 63, 65, 68
product, 68
Evaluators, 70, 71

Fiduciary control, 116
Functional fixation, 89, 90

Goals, 3-7, 27-30, 73, 110-112
appropriate,
articulation with objectives, 29
defined, 14
models of setting,
bargaining, 28
dominant coalition, 29
problem-solving, 28
types of, 27

Intuition, 102, 103

Management control, defined, 2
Management by exception, 46
Measurement, 5, 8, 76-91, 101
defined, 77
meaningfulness of, 83, 88
reliability, 86, 88
scales, 78-83, 87
specification, 84
standards, 85
types of,
derived, 86
fiat, 87
fundamental, 87
validity, 86, 88
Minimum acceptable behavior, 46
Model
defined, 77
of management control systems, 3-10

Nonempirical sciences, 99-101

Objectives, 3-7, 20, 43, 55, 64, 71, 111, 112
articulation with goals, 29
defined, 14

Operational definitions. *See* Rules of correspondence
Optimization, 18
Outputs, 3, 4, 64, 65, 107, 110

Performance, 3, 4
measures, 3-5, 38, 43, 47, 48, 54, 71, 72, 76, 78, 87, 113-115
standards, 32, 33
Planning, 5-7, 14-27, 101
contrasted to control, 18, 21
defined, 15
operational, 20, 23
as post hoc justification, 25, 112, 113
process, 15, 16, 19
strategic, 22
structure, 19, 23
tactical, 23
Plans, procedural and declarative, 16
Pragmatics, 98, 99
Preconditions, 5, 6

Resistance to change, 118
Rules of correspondence, 76, 77, 96-99

Satisficing, 18
Semantics, 98-100
Situational contingencies, 3
Staff information requirements, 117
Surrogate measures, 84, 85
Syntactics, 97, 99, 100

Technology of foolishness, 114
Theory, 76, 94-108, 110
defined, 76, 95, 97
formulation, 103
verification, 104, 107
Timing of measures, 115

Zero-based budgeting, 21, 119